# An American Patriot Manifesto

# An American Patriot Manifesto

Dave Batcheller

All other quotations have been compiled from a wide variety of sources, and are accurate to the best knowledge of the author. Any substantiated inaccuracies should be reported via email to the author at dvbatch@gmail.com and they will be revised or deleted in any future edition of this book.

# Contents

# Preface

# My Journey Continues

Just a few short years ago, I began a journey, joining millions of Americans who are deeply concerned about the direction and future of our nation. This process led me to study and rediscover our national history, heritage and form of government. Along the way, I uncovered many facts that have been suppressed or hidden from the general population through the deceptive, controlling practices of the media and our so-called leaders. By rewriting our history and manipulating the educational, judicial and political systems, those in power have led the American people into a very dark and uncertain future.

In my first book, *The Downward Spiral: Decline of the American Dream*, I targeted my message toward the mainstream of the American population. This strategy was based upon the realization that average Americans possess high levels of naiveté, ignorance, bias and apathy. Unfortunately, this is the reality of our present condition as a nation. While this new book may still serve that purpose in many ways, I am now more specifically directing my message to the growing movement of freedom-loving American patriots. My experience over the past few years has been that this movement represents simultaneously both our biggest challenge and our best hope for restoring the American dream.

As in my first book, my approach still leans toward being an easy to read, sweeping overview of complex issues. My primary intention is not to impress or rehash information that is readily available. Instead, I seek to ignite a burning fire for action, so that the crippling effects of helplessness, discouragement, fear, self-preservation and indifference will be extricated from the lives of my readers.

Throughout history, other 'manifestos' have been written – including the Communist Manifesto, the Humanist Manifesto (in several parts) and others, most referred to in this writing. These declarations outline the view and stance of a particular mindset, a public declaration of principles, intentions, motives, opinions and objectives. In the same way, I outline here the emerging view of modern patriots here in the United States of America – thus, *An American Patriot Manifesto.*

Societies are full of people who will ultimately resign themselves to follow whoever leads them – even if it is over a cliff. It is my firm conviction that we do not need an actual majority to win this struggle to restore liberty, but rather a deeply impassioned and committed minority of patriots who will not stop until greed, tyranny and globalism are eradicated from our American culture. If we are not able to awaken the American people to this cause, we may very well be witnessing the final days of our Constitutional Republic.

The United States of America today has become but a hollow shell of its former glory. We are hated or viewed with suspicion around the world. We have lost our moral compass, drifting away from the principles that this country was founded upon. Our unique culture is threatened and our economy is on the brink of collapse. What most Americans do not realize is that a greedy, power-hungry, elite group with a very clear objective - the creation and control of a global economy - is orchestrating these events. As unbelievable as it may seem, this diabolical vision requires America to be brought down from super-power status to level the world's playing field. If these people are not exposed and defeated, Americans will lose their unique history, heritage, national sovereignty and personal liberties. While most of America sleeps, this strategy is already being implemented. In reality, the scheme may be so far along that it is irreversible, unless sufficient numbers of American patriots rise up to challenge it.

As we continue our downward spiral into moral chaos and globalism, it is imperative that the American people wake up, cast off their shackles of indifference and resist this ever-increasing tyranny. Our liberty and our future are at stake. We dare not wait longer, hoping that 'someone else' will do something, or that things will just magically get better. We are living in turbulent times, as did our forefathers during the birth of this great nation. May we find within ourselves the same courage and resolve to stand up for what is right and affect the changes that are needed to preserve our Constitutional Republic.

> If ever time should come, when vain and aspiring men shall possess the highest seats in government, our country will stand in need of its experienced patriots to prevent its ruin.
> - Samuel Adams

# Chapter One

# Foundations of Liberty in America

Many Americans today are proud of their heritage, yet they do not understand our history or the principles upon which our nation was founded. This lack of knowledge has been caused, not only by time, but also by the deliberate efforts of people who are interested in controlling and reshaping our nation. Those in positions of power, who often set aside these principles, have chosen to use a slow, methodical strategy instead of outright or overnight changes. They correctly discern that most people are like sheep that will passively shift or adjust to gradual, incremental changes. Generations of Americans have come and gone since these strategies were first set into motion; and now very few of us remember where we came from, or why we became the greatest nation upon the face of the earth.

The issues debated today are very similar to the early days of our Republic - contention over the essential role or scope of government, and the sovereignty of both individuals and the States. In a very real sense, we are now reliving those tumultuous days in which men's souls were severely tested, the time which gave birth to America.

## They Came to America

While acknowledging the presence and contributions of the Native American peoples of North America, the history of the United States as a nation is vitally linked to the immigration of people from other nations. The discovery of new continents and the opportunities to explore, develop and conquer were an irresistible call to many in colonial days. Many who came to America were fleeing religious persecution; some were escaping political oppression; and others were merely seeking a chance at prosperity or a fresh start in the New World. By the thousands, they poured into the Americas, embarking on a new adventure that many hoped would be their Promised Land. In the beginning, they mostly came from Europe, but eventually they would come from Africa, Asia, and every corner of the globe.

## The Search for True Liberty

As the American colonists labored to carve out a new way of life in North America, the unique challenges and obstacles that they faced shaped their character. These pioneers became strong and independent by surviving and overcoming adversity. Their ingenuity and productivity were unrivaled, and as time passed, the fires of liberty and independence began to grow in their hearts.

The years leading up to the American Revolution were filled with strife, turmoil, oppression and spiritual renewal. The British Empire was the most powerful and expansive colonial power on the planet and its leaders were determined to protect and extend their empire. At the same time, the quest for true freedom grew stronger in the hearts of the American colonists with each passing year. This was a collision of colossal magnitude in the making! Each attempt by the British Crown to oppress or control the colonists only added fuel to the fires of resistance and independence. Eventually, the smoldering embers of liberty would ignite into a full-blown rebellion against tyranny, the effects of which would forever shake and reshape North America and the world.

## Remembering our Roots

To really understand the founding of America, we must first gain at least an elementary grasp of certain historical and ideological truths. Disconnecting us from our past is one of the chief strategies of those who are intent on reshaping our nation.

We must not allow ourselves to be stripped of our history and heritage, even though parts of it were indeed ugly or revealed the evil tendencies within human nature.

If we wish to continue to be a free people, it is imperative that we comprehend our actual history and resist the rewritten fables that many propose today. Our responsibilities as American citizens are to uphold the principles of liberty, honor and integrity; to discern the difference between lies and incontrovertible facts; and to constantly strive together for improvement and to be a positive influence in the world.

To gain this foundational understanding of America's roots, we need to be aware of certain persons whose lives and teachings shaped our nation. There was, of course, a multitude of people who contributed to the founding of America. Yet to provide a basic overview, we will now consider some of the primary issues, key players and events.

## A Blending of Ideas

The birthing of America took place over a long period, as well-educated men pondered and formulated a vision for a new society. Their views drew heavily from elements of Greek, Roman, Anglo-Saxon, continental European and English history and thought.

Polybius was a Greek philosopher who lived in the second century B.C., during the transitional time of the Roman conquest of the Greek Empire. He advocated blending the strengths of various common forms of government, dividing the powers into three self-balancing branches. Even though he saw the early developments of these ideas within the Roman Empire, they were soon abandoned in favor of having an emperor, which resulted in the rise of the Caesars.

Marcus Tullius Cicero was a Roman from the first century B.C., whose innovative ideas often dissected the frequently confusing or contradictory philosophies of Plato and Aristotle. Cicero's main premise became known as 'Natural Law,' meaning that a Supreme Creator had instituted certain elements of divine order, human conscience, and reasoning. He also proposed laws based on principles of justice and morality. Cicero was one of the favorites of America's Founding Fathers. His thought is clearly reflected in Thomas Jefferson's language within the *Declaration of Independence*, which states:

> When in the course of human events, it becomes necessary for one people to dissolve the political bands which have connected them with another, and to assume among the powers of the earth, the separate and equal station to which the Laws of Nature and of Nature's God entitle them, a decent respect to the opinions of mankind requires that they should declare the causes which impel them to the separation.
>
> We hold these truths to be self-evident, that all men are created equal, that they are endowed by their Creator with certain unalienable rights; that among these are life, liberty and the pursuit of happiness - that to secure these rights, governments are instituted among men, deriving their just powers from the consent of the governed.

Another integral part of America's foundation was the principles found in Anglo-Saxon Common Law, which were later connected with the practices of ancient Israel in the biblical time of Moses. In 1639, the Reverend Thomas Hooker wrote the *Fundamental Orders of Connecticut*, which became the first written constitution of modern times. Hooker articulated the principles of Moses in the first chapter of Deuteronomy as a model for a new form of government. The primary points of Common Law are represented by the following list.

- The people considered themselves to be a commonwealth of freemen.
- There was an over-arching, well-known belief that rights and laws originated from God.
- These individual rights were considered unalienable and sacred.
- Personal responsibility was a central and widely accepted reality.
- This responsibility extended out through the family, tribe, state and nation, in that order.
- Decisions were made by vote or by consensus, with the consent of the people.
- Power was dispersed or decentralized; not focused on one person or a small group.
- Society was organized into small, manageable groups, upwards from the local level.
- There was a strong moral code established, with strict adherence and enforcement.
- All efforts were made to resolve problems at the same level in which they originated.
- Further or higher level resolutions would only be sought if this approach did not work.

You can see from this list how these principles were blended together in the development of America's unique approach to government. This focus ensured that individual rights and responsibility would never be lost or shifted away from the people. Any deviation from these principles or concentration of power elsewhere would be met with resistance from the established laws and the voice of the people itself. At least that was the original intention.

Years later, a committee consisting of Thomas Jefferson, John Adams, and Benjamin Franklin proposed an official seal for the United States of America. Their original proposal was to show (on the two sides of the seal) the connection between ancient Israel and the Anglo Saxon view of Common Law.

## Our Judeo-Christian Heritage

One of the primary considerations left out in most modern renditions of our nations' founding was the heavy influence of Judeo-Christian teaching. Despite mounting efforts to separate faith from public life and remove all mention of God, it is quite clear that this heritage was prevalent in the early days of our Republic. Personal faith and a basic moral code, as outlined in the Bible, provided a solid foundation for our society.

This strong emphasis of religion can still be seen across the land, and is exemplified by synagogues and churches of all kinds, as well as monuments, landmarks and the names of cities and places everywhere. There are inscriptions on most of our government buildings that quote the Bible, the Ten Commandments and other religious pictures or sayings. These include the U.S Capitol, Supreme Court, Library of Congress, National Archives, Washington Monument, the Jefferson and Lincoln Memorials and the White House. Another great example is the Liberty Bell in Philadelphia, inscribed with a verse from Leviticus 25:10, which reads, "Proclaim liberty throughout all the land unto all the inhabitants thereof."

In America, even the existence and practice of other religious faiths is not only permitted, but also protected under the Constitution. Hindus, Buddhists, Jews, Muslims and other religions are allowed to practice their faith here, alongside many variations of the Christian faith. The reality of this freedom, however, does not change our historical roots.

In colonial America, and in the hearts of our Founding Fathers, the importance of the Bible and the teachings of Jesus were universally respected and admired. This stands in stark contrast to our present use of humanistic teaching, political correctness, multiculturalism and anti-God rhetoric. People then viewed their rights as coming directly from God – not the king, the government, or anywhere else. In addition, they believed that God placed these rights into the hearts of men with 'self-evident truths' - an innate sense of right and wrong. These individual rights were to be combined with a mutual respect for our fellow citizens. Consider these comments regarding the role of government:

> The state's most fundamental duty is to protect citizens from the sinful conduct of their neighbors. The Bible indicates that government is to act to preserve order – people's ability to live "peaceful and quiet lives," in Paul's words – in a sinful world. The state is to be a godly agent that not only allows men to follow God but also contains the harm that would occur were there no public constraints on evil behavior.
> – Michael Cromartie, *Caesar's Coin Revisited*

The responsibility of government is not to take care of us or solve our personal problems. Nor is it to regulate or control every aspect of our lives. The Judeo-Christian beliefs of our Founding Fathers led them to believe that government was instituted primarily to serve the common good of the people, to promote justice and righteousness, to dispense just retribution, and to serve as a neutral arbiter and protector of the people. In other words, to protect "life, liberty and the pursuit of happiness" and to enable people to enjoy God's blessings.

> Do not pervert justice; do not show partiality to the poor or favoritism to the great, but judge your neighbor fairly. - Leviticus 19:15

**Separation of Church and State?**

The recent, distorted view of the 'separation of church and state' was not something in the minds or hearts of our Founding Fathers. Even though their personal beliefs varied, there was still a general sense of unity and conviction regarding the teachings of the Christian faith.

The idea of the Founders was not to prohibit or regulate religion, but rather to allow people of any faith to practice what they believe without government interference or regulation. This search for true liberty had led many from Europe to flee religious oppression and persecution. The actual intent of the Founders was to safeguard this fundamental right – in other words, to protect the church from the government!

The development of the false teaching of separation of church from state parallels the moral and governmental decline in our culture over the past several generations.

> In the hands of an elite group of reformers this amendment is now being turned on its head in a way that would make its original authors wince. Today our courts often interpret freedom *of* religion as freedom *from* religion. Rather than separating the church from state interference, the meaning now is that religious practices should be ousted from the state. Powerful forces are seeking to uproot every vestige of Christian influence, rewrite our history, and banish God from the public sector. – Erwin Lutzer, *Hitler's Cross*

> Today the separation of church and state in America is used to silence the church. When Christians speak out on issues, the hue and cry from the humanist state and media is that Christians, and all religions, are prohibited from speaking since there is a separation of church and state. The way the concept is used today is totally reversed from the original intent. It is not rooted in history… Pluralism has come to mean that everything is acceptable. This new concept of pluralism suddenly is everywhere. There is no right or wrong; it is just a matter of your personal preference.
> – Francis Schaeffer, *A Christian Manifesto*

**Laying the Foundation**

For centuries, Europe had been dominated by monarchies that were heavily influenced or even controlled by state religions. As England, France, Spain and other nations colonized much of the world during the fifteenth and sixteenth centuries, a particular view of government began to emerge. Even as the fires of Reformation swept through Europe, challenging the traditions and teaching of the Roman Catholic Church, so new political ideologies began to surface that would eventually lead to a completely new form of government in America. Over time, the American colonies became a place where these new ideas would take root and flourish.

One of the men who dramatically shaped this new philosophy was the Reverend Samuel Rutherford, a Scottish Presbyterian theologian and author. In 1644, Rutherford penned a book entitled *Lex Rex: the Law and the Prince*. In this treatise, he exposed the fallacies of what was commonly known as 'the divine right of kings,' meaning that a certain elite class of people possessed inherently a special place or right from God Himself to rule over their subjects. The kings owned and controlled all territory within what was known as their 'realm' and the people were subjects, with no rights to property or personal liberty. In this reality, the governments of men were based on the power and whims of those who possessed this status.

Throughout his life, Rutherford expounded the theories of limited government, the separation of powers, the rule of law and constitutionalism. His book was later banned and burned by the authorities, and he was convicted of high treason. Rutherford died, however, before his sentence of execution was carried out.

Another well-known philosopher and political writer who heavily influenced our Founding Fathers was the Englishman, John Locke. His ideas about natural rights, labor, property, and government were also considered quite revolutionary for his time. Locke's arguments concerning liberty and the theory of a 'social contract' between people and their government later influenced the views of Alexander Hamilton, James Madison, Thomas Jefferson, Benjamin Franklin and many others. Locke took many of Rutherford's ideas and put them in a more secular context. Some of America's founders, like Jefferson and Franklin, who were later considered to be Deists, were more in line with Locke's views.

Closer to the time of the American Revolution was Sir William Blackstone, an English jurist and professor, who produced the historical and analytic treatise on Common Law called *Commentaries on the Laws of England*, first published in four volumes from 1765–1769. These volumes became the definitive source of Common Law thought in America, often cited by the Founding Fathers, as well as the U.S. Courts, for many years.

In 1776, Scottish economist Adam Smith published his landmark *The Wealth of Nations*, which advocated a free market economy as being more productive and beneficial to society. This work also contributed greatly to the emerging principles of the American society and government.

John Witherspoon was a Presbyterian minister and president of what is now Princeton University. A devoted student of Rutherford, he was the only pastor to sign the Declaration of Independence. Immediately after the American War for Independence was over, Congress called for the first official Thanksgiving Day to give thanks to God. Witherspoon's speech on that day reflected his perspective and that of America's founders. In that famous speech, he declared:

> A republic once equally poised must either preserve its virtue or lose its liberty.
> - John Witherspoon

Men like Baron Charles de Montesquieu of France also influenced the developing thought of the American framers significantly. Montesquieu became famous for his theory of the separation of powers. His landmark philosophical writing called *The Spirit of Laws* became one of the most important political works of the eighteenth century and included ideas for a model constitution.

## Choosing a Form of Government

Our Founding Fathers thoroughly contemplated all the various forms of human government prior to forming our Republic here in America. Along the way, they considered monarchies, aristocracies, oligarchies, dictatorships, democracies and republics. They did not embark on this journey lightly or on a whim. Their course was uncharted territory every step of the way, and the results in terms of human history were not only unique, but also quite remarkable, bearing the very fingerprint of divine providence, wisdom and guidance.

By way of stark contrast, the French Revolution, which occurred shortly after the American Revolution, resulted in tremendous upheaval, chaos and the Napoleonic Wars because these principles were not firmly rooted in the foundation. The results and development of both nations clearly demonstrate the effects of following or applying these foundational principles of liberty.

## Further Refinement of these Thoughts in America

Highly educated and astute, the emerging leaders of the American colonies began to develop these ideas even further. Men like John Adams, Benjamin Franklin, Thomas Jefferson, James Madison, George Washington and a host of others, forged ahead in their pursuit of the American dream. Theory began to take tangible shape as they wrestled with all the options or alternatives. As pressure came upon them in the form of British tyranny, their determination to implement these principles grew stronger each year.

In his book *The 5000 Year Leap*, Cleon Skousen summarized the brilliance of these men:

> Part of the genius of the Founding Fathers was their political spectrum or political frame of reference. It was a yardstick for the measuring of the political power in any particular system of government. They had a much better political yardstick than the one which is generally used today. If the Founders had used the modern yardstick of 'Communism on the left' and 'Fascism on the right,' they would never have found the balanced center which they were seeking.

Central to the debate from the beginning was the authority or role of each colony and any proposed federal government, as well as the rights of individual citizens. Some Americans leaned toward a strong centralized government, which others opposed vehemently. There were even some who advocated returning to a monarchy, eventually proposing to make George Washington the first king!

In due course, these two general camps became known as the Federalists and the Anti-Federalists. *The Federalist Papers*, a collection of essays penned by James Madison, Alexander Hamilton and John Jay, became the focal point of the ongoing debate as our nation struggled to find the balance of powers.

On this anvil of debate, Americans forged the path to liberty and a new form of government. Their diverse views frequently created disagreement, tension and even conflict. Yet through all of this, a clear direction slowly began to materialize. Then, as the pressure cooker of British oppression intensified, they together found a way to resolve their differences and stand unified against their common foe.

## Igniting the Fires of Liberty and Independence

Always present in the emerging direction of our Founding Fathers was their belief that God intended to use America as an example and blessing to the entire world. This conviction was rooted in their understanding of scripture and a deep sense of divine providence and calling. This sense of purpose, or 'manifest destiny' as it was later called, was a strong unifying and motivating factor in America's early development.

As British repression increased, the American colonists gradually became more determined and direct in their response. Appeals, petitions and demonstrations began to give way to events such as the Boston Tea Party, the defiance of British legislation or edicts and the sinking of British ships. Men found themselves facing the sword of totalitarianism and their otherwise peaceful and diplomatic natures began to morph into a fierce determination to uphold the principles of liberty, which they had come to embrace wholeheartedly. Eventually they were drawn into full-scale warfare in defense of their liberties and their nation.

Independence was achieved in America through the efforts of many people. Notable among the many that helped ignite the American Revolution were patriots like Samuel Adams, Paul Revere, Patrick Henry and Thomas Paine.

Yes, Samuel Adams was a brewer, but also a statesman and politician who became one of the most outspoken and prominent catalysts of the American Revolution. Adams, second cousin to our second president John Adams, was a fiery, determined patriot who wrote many essays, lobbied, appealed and mobilized the people through groups like the Sons of Liberty.

Paul Revere was a silversmith by trade who was also active in the Sons of Liberty. He later helped organize an intelligence and alarm system to keep watch on the British military. Revere became famous for his 'midnight ride' to warn the citizens of Lexington and Concord, Massachusetts of the impending confiscation of their weapons.

Patrick Henry, a member of the Sons of Liberty and the first governor of Virginia, is remembered as one of the most influential (and radical) advocates of the American Revolution. He was especially forthright in support of republicanism and in his denunciations of corruption and the unethical behavior of government officials. In the midst of division and indecisiveness, his fiery speech of 1775 in the House of Burgesses in Richmond, Virginia impassioned and mobilized the people against the encroaching British army.

In 1776, Thomas Paine wrote and distributed a pamphlet entitled *Common Sense*, a powerful, widely read attack on British tyranny. This call for American independence, initially called *The Plain Truth*, was written in a simple, logical format that fueled the flames of liberty across the American colonies.

That same year, under threat of reprisals for treason, 56 brave men affixed their names to the *Declaration of Independence*, declaring in conclusion:

> And for the support of this Declaration, with a firm reliance on the protection of Divine Providence, we mutually pledge to each other our Lives, our Fortunes, and our sacred Honor.

Without people like this, who were willing to take a firm stand and lay their lives on the line, American independence and liberty would not have been achieved. We must never forget the determination and sacrifice of the brave patriots who stood firm against all odds to bring our nation into existence!

The foundations of liberty in America were established upon solid principles derived from the blending of ideas that spanned many centuries. Until fairly recently, Americans have regarded this foundation as being vitally connected to their religious faith and the blessing or favor of God.

> America's founders, irrespective of their individual faith commitments, established a limited national government of enumerated powers because their shared biblical worldview warned them against the danger of mixing sinful human nature and concentrated political authority. They saw a Constitution that restricted and decentralized state power as the only way to

> protect people from the actions of ruthless, greedy, self-serving rulers.
> – Michael Cromartie, *Caesar's Coin Revisited*

The results of this strong foundation carved a unique place for the United States of America in the history of the world. The rest of the world, generally speaking, has been enriched, inspired and blessed in many different ways by the emergence of our Republic.

# Chapter Two

# The Long Road to Tyranny

The American colonists had been here for well over a hundred years before British domination became an unbearable weight. As the English Empire expanded, so did the demands on their colonies. Ultimately, these demands became intolerable and unacceptable.

Since securing independence, the United States has enjoyed the benefits of our unique system of government for well over 200 years. We have also suffered, however, a gradual decline in morality, citizen responsibility and the values upon which our nation was originally founded. The vision of our Founding Fathers is now clouded and in jeopardy. Our Constitution is on the verge of extinction due to gradual changes in our culture, economy and political system. We are once again facing a national crisis, a crossroads on the long road to tyranny, which threatens not only our personal liberties, but also the future of our Republic.

**Forming a More Perfect Union**

Any honest rendition of our nation's founding will acknowledge that there was an internal struggle from the beginning to determine the type of government that we would have in the United States. Because human nature is constant and history often repeats itself, we have witnessed the incremental moral decline and encroachment of government about which our Founding Fathers warned us.

> Yes, we did produce a near perfect Republic. But will they keep it, or will they, in the enjoyment of

> plenty, lose the memory of freedom? Material abundance without character is the surest way to destruction. - Thomas Jefferson

> We have no government armed in power capable of contending in human passions unbridled by morality and religion. Our constitution was made only for a moral and religious people. It is wholly inadequate for the government of any other.
> - John Adams, address to the militia of Massachusetts, 1798

In the midst of war with England, the Americans floundered in their pursuit of independence. The colonial army was severely outgunned and undersupplied. As for the colonial government, its reactionary emphasis initially leaned too far in one direction, with virtually no central or national powers. In 1777, the Continental Congress adopted the *First Articles of Confederation.* Although this was an improvement, the Articles granted so few powers to the federal government that in a short time our fledgling nation was teetering on the edge of survival. This approach underestimated the need for legitimate federal powers and proved to be wholly inadequate. Our Founding Fathers therefore soon found themselves in serious need of regrouping and refining their approach.

Through no small miracle and after eight long years, the colonials achieved ultimate victory on the battlefield and American independence was secured. In 1787, a Constitutional Convention was called and the U.S. Constitution was drafted and ratified. After a long, arduous war and seemingly endless internal debate, the Americans were finally able to find a balance between the state and federal roles in government.

## The Seeds of Corruption

Even in the midst of the miracle that became America, there were problems. The seeds of corruption, found within human nature itself, were present from the beginning. It should come as no surprise that even the best plans conceived by man will ultimately succumb to a process of deterioration and death. This lesson can be seen clearly by a careful study of American history.

> The framers of the Constitution made the faulty assumption that We the People would keep close watch over the government because it was in our best interest to do so. I am ashamed to say that most Americans haven't got a clue about what the Constitution actually says. If We the People want to claim our rights, we must also claim final responsibility for what happens in Washington, D.C. If you vote for the 'lesser of two evils' and your candidate wins, you still end up with evil.
> – Michael Badnarik, *Good to Be King*

The best government in the world is subject to the imperfections of human nature, and this is true of our nation's leaders throughout history. Badnarik goes on to illustrate this:

> Corruption in our government started even before the ink was dry on the Constitution. Alexander Hamilton was a nationalist who called himself a federalist. John Adams enacted the Alien and Sedition Act that made it illegal to publicly criticize the government. Andrew Jackson used 'eminent domain' to justify possession of Indian territory from a race of people who did not comprehend the idea of claiming air, water or land as private property.

> However, the first president to blatantly violate the spirit of the Constitution was Abraham Lincoln. He was the first to misinterpret the Constitution in order to claim 'extraordinary war powers.' His quest was to keep the union together using whatever force was necessary. By what logic do you decide to save a nation by ignoring the principle that created it? Lincoln's motives may have been pure, but that does not absolve him from the crime of exceeding his limited executive powers.
>
> Although Lincoln may have strayed from the Constitution, the president who gets my vote for most corrupt and evil is Franklin Delano Roosevelt. FDR used the panic of the Great Depression as a justification for establishing our deeply entrenched welfare system, which is obviously socialism to those of us who understand the sanctity of private property.
> - Michael Badnarik, *Good to Be King*

**Early Signs of Deterioration**

From the earliest days of our Republic, some believed strongly in a very powerful federal government and a centralized banking system. This direction was resisted by those faithful to the Constitution and the vision of our Founding Fathers for many years, yet the internal struggle was always very real.

While confronting a massive push toward centralized banking, President Andrew Jackson responded with fierce, determined opposition. His courage and firm resolve held off the devouring tendencies of the bankers.

Some years later, as he faced the crises of a nation divided and a mounting war debt, President Abraham Lincoln emerged as an enigma in American history. On one hand, Lincoln clearly understood the dangers of centralized banking and gave lip service to the Constitution. At the same time, for sake of expediency and his own agenda, he was willing to abandon the Constitution and implement changes that would make our Founders shudder. Does that sound familiar?

> The Civil War years saw the rapid centralization and enlargement of the federal government. Taxes were imposed upon most manufactured goods, tariff rates were increased, and an inheritance tax was adopted. During that period, the first personal income tax in the history of the United States was imposed …
> - Andrew Napolitano, *The Constitution in Exile*

**Further Erosion of Our Republic**

The twentieth century brought a continuation of this descending path, with all three branches of government contributing to the decline. Certain presidents, like Woodrow Wilson, Franklin D. Roosevelt and Lyndon Johnson, all kicked open the floodgates to socialism in America. The Supreme Court contributed significantly by ignoring our historical rule of law, by reinterpreting the law and by redesigning the entire judicial system right before our eyes. Congress has been complicit as well by refusing to follow the Constitution and hold the other branches of government in check.

America has been led into this federal domination by manipulation and secret back room deals. The creation of the Federal Reserve Bank, along with the alleged passage of the 16th Amendment, brought America into centralized banking and personal income taxation. The introduction of massive, government-controlled welfare programs under FDR brought us into socialism. The Great Depression and two World Wars were used as an excuse and a disguise. The failed League of Nations was eventually replaced by the United Nations, which, along with many other organizations such as the World Bank, the World Health Organization and others, set the stage for further pursuits of globalism. Our blame has been to sit idly by and believe the lies.

## Behind the Scenes

Most Americans are not aware of the history or impact that many people or groups have had on our country from behind the scenes. Family banking dynasties, like the Medicis, Fuggers and the Rothschilds have dominated the world of finance for centuries. As these trends spread to America, major conglomerates such as M.M. Warburg & Co., the Bank of England, the Rockefellers and Standard Oil Co., J.P. Morgan, Chase Bank, Kuhn-Loeb & Co. and others have extended their tentacles across the land.

Intertwined with the banking powers are clandestine societies that have shrouded their activities and influence in relative secrecy. Among others, these groups include the Illuminati, the Freemasons, the Skull and Bones Society, the Bilderberg Group, the Council on Foreign Relations, and the Trilateral Commission. Attempts to expose the influence that these groups exert upon government have often been branded as 'conspiracy theories' in order to draw attention away from them. The result is that these societies remain relatively unknown or misunderstood by the public. We are told with disdain that these organizations are harmless and any attempt to expose their true nature is done by wild-eyed fanatics. Their long existence and influence, as well as their connections and secrets, are never explained however. To any person who probes beyond the surface, there are obvious overlapping, commingled purposes and objectives. In reality, these groups have asserted a disproportionate amount of influence upon our government.

**Exposing the Federal Reserve**

Many feel that the heart of the beast that threatens our Republic is the Federal Reserve Bank. Contrary to popular understanding, this banking cartel is NOT a part of the U.S. government; rather it is a private corporation controlled by an elite group of world bankers. It creates money out of thin air and then loans it back to the United States government while charging interest! Their ultimate goal is to manipulate and control the world's economy.

The very existence of the Federal Reserve is a clear abandonment of the Constitution and government responsibility. Even though the President appoints the chairman of the Fed, with Congressional approval, the Constitution does not give the President or Congress the authority to abdicate their powers to another branch or agency. Moreover, the decisions and practices of the Fed are not ratified or monitored by the government. They have never been audited, a fact which by itself should lead us to great suspicion. Our government itself has become a slave of the Federal Reserve.

The Federal Reserve claims that nobody owns it. Yet it has centralized control of the American banking system through twelve regional banks and the ownership of these banks is clouded in secrecy. To make matters worse, Congress has repeatedly given the Fed autonomy to carry out its day-to-day operations with insulation from political pressure or accountability.

In order to free the American people, the history and operations of the Federal Reserve must be exposed and then it must be completely eradicated from the United States!

## Don't Get in the Way of 'Progress'

A web of deception has frequently veiled the movement and decisions of our national leaders. Through disguised legislation, behind the scene deals and outright fraud and corruption, Americans have been duped into allowing fundamental changes to our original ideals. Even while we have been willing to sacrifice, fight and die for our country, we have been misled, taken advantage of, and had our rights gradually stripped from us, in layers so fine that on a day to day basis it has been difficult to notice.

Over the years, our federal government has gradually and systematically expanded, consuming more and more of America's land, resources and liberties. Federal land grabs have resulted in a huge percentage of American soil being owned and controlled by either our own government or by foreigners. At the same time, international banking and trade deals have sold off vast numbers of American jobs and business interests to foreign nations or companies. What we are told is exactly what the authorities want us to believe.

> As more jobs go overseas, the United States stands to lose the most economically successful middle class in the history of the world.
> –Jerome Corsi, *The Late Great USA*

## And Here We Are

In the minds of many, Ronald Reagan was the last American president to uphold traditional American values. However, even he was inconsistent at times and failed to stop the overwhelming tide of secularism, humanism and liberalism. Of course, no one person could be blamed for this tidal wave of compromise and filth. Many other politicians, the courts, the church, and ultimately every American who remained silent or stood idly by are all partly responsible for where we are today.

The subsequent presidencies of both Bushes, sandwiched around that of Bill Clinton, have taken our nation to new lows. America was prepared for the entrance of globalism and the New World Order, the office of the president was shamefully disgraced, and our nation was led into a volatile 'war on terror' under false pretenses. All three continued to violate the Constitution at every turn, yet despite their presumed power and influence, they were mere puppets carrying out the wishes of an unseen, mysterious shadow government.

Now, with Barack Obama as president, we have blasted into turbo-speed and are now rapidly sinking into the abyss of socialism and a complete disregard for the Constitution. If this is not stopped, we will soon witness a true and total 'American Makeover.' It seems quite clear that the vast majority of American politicians and general populace care not one bit about the fact that Barack Obama cannot (or will not) produce a valid birth certificate to prove that he is a natural born U.S. citizen. His personal history, training, policies and vision for American are all a culmination and a further extension of this slide into tyranny.

As we enter the twenty first century, America finds herself floundering with complex problems, many of which are our own creation. Financial stupidity and mismanagement have led us to the brink of economic collapse. An inconsistent, over-extended foreign policy puts our people at serious risk. And rising internal strife now threatens to divide America. As our government attempts to deal with these many issues, we find ourselves racing at breakneck speed toward becoming a totalitarian police state. The vibration you may feel under your feet is our Founding Fathers turning in their graves.

**Trading Liberty for Security?**

In this post 9/11 world, our leaders frequently attempt to manipulate us, through deception and fear, into exchanging our God-given rights for government provision, protection and security. We must recognize this exchange for what it really is – simply a means to control us. In the process, they will always bleed us for every dollar they can get to fund their programs and line their own pockets. This is what leeches and parasites do. It is in their very nature. We must never tire of exposing and resisting them!

> Those who give up essential liberties for temporary safety deserve neither liberty nor safety. - Benjamin Franklin

**Eerie Parallels with Hitler's Germany**

Many have noted the significant parallels to the rise of Nazi Germany that are increasingly observable in the United States. This of course will come as a shock to many Americans who naively cling to the notion that we would never allow this to happen here. While we may be lacking the impetus of a major national crisis at this moment, we are nonetheless marching down a similar path. It is only a matter of time until the crisis comes.

> Hitler considered himself the superman of Nietzsche's philosophy. He rejoiced that the doctrine of God that had always stood in the way of brutality and deceit had now been removed. Once man had replaced God, the way was clear for Nietzsche's super race led by a superman to dominate the world.
>
> Perhaps now we can better understand the concentration camps. Ideas do have

> consequences, and the notion that God was dead freed humans to do as they pleased. With God cast down, man was free to rise up and pursue his unrestrained lust for power … It has been said that after God died in the nineteenth century, man died in the twentieth. For when God is dead, man becomes an untamed beast.
> – Erwin Lutzer, *Hitler's Cross*

Adolf Hitler seized an opportunity following Germany's loss in World War I and the subsequent Great Inflation, to play upon the fears of the German people. He aroused their sense of national destiny and rallied them around promises of security, change, restoration and greatness. He did this while at the same time stripping them of their faith and morality. The multitudes, oblivious to what was really going on, were led blindly down a path to totalitarianism and slaughter.

Here in America, rapid increases in security and surveillance measures, suppression of dissidents, unelected officials that dictate important national policy and vast government programs designed to further inhibit our personal liberties, have all become pervasive throughout the United States. The American people are also, for the most part, asleep and compliant, as were the German people in that era.

## Stopping the Slide into Tyranny

> Does government fear us? Or do we fear the government? When the people fear the government, tyranny has found victory. The government is our servant, not our master!
> - Thomas Jefferson

In the mind of Jefferson, and many of our Founding Fathers, the existence and reality of this tension required constant vigilance by We, the People and our willing defense of liberty at all costs. Otherwise, the evil and corruption within human nature, manifested through human governments, would eventually strip us of our liberties and threaten our unalienable rights.

> The tree of liberty must be refreshed from time to time with the blood of patriots and tyrants.
> - Thomas Jefferson

# Chapter Three

# A Nation Adrift

> There is an alternative to national bankruptcy, a bigger police state, trillion dollar wars, and a government that draws ever more parasitically on the productive energies of the American people. It's called freedom.
> – Ron Paul, *The Revolution: A Manifesto*

**Adrift in a Turbulent Sea**

America has become like a ship lost at sea, driven by fierce winds, storms and shifting currents. We have lost our way. In these turbulent times, we have forgotten where we came from and we are unsure of where we are going. Instead of dreaming, pioneering and inventing, most of us live in survival mode, simply reacting to what happens around us. Our many advances, breakthroughs and technologies have not delivered us from anxiety, fear or pain. We have taken on this survival mentality because we can no longer see the land that our ancestors dreamed of so long ago. Our strength, courage and moral fortitude have been stretched nearly to the limit, and our enemies are standing just outside the door.

Along our American journey, we have encountered many storms that have tested our character and our values. We have faced these storms with remarkable strength and resilience. Yet over the years our eyesight has become blurred, our convictions eroded, and our resolve seriously weakened. Our responses to changes in the world, and the incremental advances of government oppression have taken their toll.

We have also been frequently raided by pirates and attacked by sharks – ambitious, greedy and unscrupulous men who only seek greater wealth and power for themselves. We have become their subjects, enslaved in every sense of the word. Yet many of us do not perceive this, because it has been veiled in deception. At the mercy of the wind and waves, we continue on, facing the perils of the sea. Oppressed and attacked at every turn, we struggle on with the feeble hope that somehow things will get better.

With no anchor and a broken compass, America is now drifting into the fog of an uncertain future. Paralyzed by relativism and political correctness, we are no longer able to tell the difference between right and wrong. We have lost both our mooring and our sense of purpose and direction. Feebly grasping at the memories of former greatness, the United States of America now struggles to find its place in a different world.

> Without question, America is different post 9/11. We live in a time of fear. Soon after the tragic events of that horrible day, the USA Patriot Act was quickly cobbled together. Unfortunately, in our fear, we allowed the final version of the act to pass despite the fact that it is directly and profoundly offensive to our Constitution …
>
> … Those in government do not feel constrained by the Constitution. They think they can do whatever they want. They have hired vast teams of government lawyers to twist and torture the plain meaning of the Fourth Amendment to justify their aggrandizement of power to themselves.
> – Andrew Napolitano, *The Constitution in Exile*

## Too Much Gray

Today's world is filled with gray. It is becoming increasingly difficult to see black or white - to tell right from wrong. Moral absolutes have yielded to relativism. American values and ideals have succumbed to endless compromise and political correctness. Bombarded each day with lies, deception and scandals, we have become numb and calloused. To make matters even worse, most of us have chosen to look the other way.

> Americans have grown weary of their responsibilities, and our government has been only too eager to relieve us of those burdens... By allowing the government to assume our responsibilities, we have gradually given away many of our rights.
> – Michael Badnarik, *Good to Be King*

## Playing the Shell Game

The daily escapades of those in power often remind me of playing the shell game. You know - the game where someone deftly maneuvers three shells so fast that you can't remember which one contains the hidden stone? The movements and changes are so swift and deceptive that a normal person can't keep up.

Is it our economy ... or our foreign policy? Maybe it's politics ... some new crisis ... or a possible terrorist threat? Who knows? We are kept guessing and distracted, while all along those controlling the game continue to unfold their backroom deals and predetermined schemes. The rest of us become dizzy and just keep trying to pay the bills.

**The Life Cycle of Great Cultures**

There is a predictable end to a society that loses its way in this fog. History shows us this repeatedly. Every great empire eventually fell apart and was conquered. Do we dare think that America is immune? Babylon, Egypt, the Mayans, Incas, and Aztecs, China, Greece, Rome, the Soviet Union and many other regimes have crumbled, either from internal decay, or by being overrun by an emerging, stronger power.

When the nation of Israel reached the bottom of this terrible cycle, the prophets rose up at different times to declare to the people:

> Woe to those who call evil good, and good evil; who substitute darkness for light and light for darkness; who substitute bitter for sweet, and sweet for bitter! - Isaiah 5:20

> Woe to him who builds his house without righteousness and his upper rooms without justice, who uses his neighbors' services without pay and does not give him his wages ... But your eyes and your heart are intent only upon your dishonest gain, and on shedding innocent blood and on practicing oppression and extortion.
> – Jeremiah 22:13, 17

> In you they have taken bribes to shed blood; you have taken interest and profits, and you have injured your neighbors for gain by oppression, and you have forgotten me, declares the Lord God. – Ezekiel 22:12

> Yes, destruction and violence are before me; strife exists and contention arises, therefore, the law is

> ignored and justice is never upheld, for the wicked surround the righteous; therefore justice comes out perverted. – Habakkuk 1:3-4

Today, our leaders frequently resort to tactics of deception and fear to manipulate us into allowing their schemes. They prey upon our natural weaknesses. This behavior from the top causes others to behave in like manner. Our land then becomes filled with injustice and oppression! No longer inspired to greatness and the high road, we are gradually swallowed up by our base instincts.

> The alternative consists of an ever-growing financial burden, more police state measures, and an endless string of wars, pitched to Americans on the basis of now-familiar propaganda and financed by more borrowing, higher taxes, and more money printed out of thin air. The collapse of the dollar will not be far behind.
>
> The empire game our government has been playing is coming to an end one way or another. This is the fate of all empires: they overextend themselves and then suffer a financial catastrophe, typically involving the destruction of the currency. – Ron Paul, *The Revolution: A Manifesto*

**America on the Brink**

Our legal, financial and governmental institutions can only keep our system propped up for so long. History and common sense both scream out the warning signals of a system stretched to the breaking point.

> A society becomes totalitarian when its structure becomes flagrantly artificial. That is when its

> ruling class has lost its function but succeeds in clinging to power by force or fraud.
> – George Orwell, *The Prevention of Literature*

At the core of this artificial, corrupt system, we find the root of the problem – lust and greed; a thirst for power and control that is insatiable and consumes all in its path.

> Power tends to corrupt, and absolute power corrupts absolutely. Great men are almost always bad men. – Lord Acton, in a letter to Bishop Mandell Creighton, 1887

This corruption is so deep in Washington, D.C. that it now trickles down to the state and local levels all over the country.

> That is the core of the issue of Congress bribing the states. Congress is empowered under the Constitution to tax and spend, but the Court has found that "incident to this power, Congress may attach conditions to the receipt of the federal funds…"

> You are probably thinking that if bribery of federal officials is illegal, then bribery by federal official should be illegal. How can members of Congress bribe state officials? The point of the federal bribery statute is that they cannot! Yet conditioning the receipt of federal funds on complying with Congress's wishes is essentially bribery with a constitutional fig leaf.
> - Andrew Napolitano, *The Constitution in Exile*

In order to compensate for their own failures and ineptitude, attorneys, judges and government officials resort to punishing the innocent and enabling the lawbreakers. Our financial system, our law enforcement agencies and our judicial system have become extremely convoluted. More and more, Draconian government regulations and taxes are layered upon us. The results are tighter restrictions and suffocating violations of our personal rights.

> Government is not the solution to our problems.
> Government is the problem.
> – President Ronald Reagan

This is why we are headed for a national disaster, and why our only real hope is to clean the government house completely and reestablish Constitutional governance in our nation. Anything less will only prolong our agony and strengthen the chains of our slavery.

> Today we are facing the possibility that the United States of America may not long endure. Our national sovereignty is in danger of being compromised in favor of an emerging regional government, designed of the elite, by the elite, and for the elite, who are working to achieve global ambitions in the pursuit of wealth and power for themselves. – Jerome Corsi, *The Late Great USA*

**Charting a New Course**

It is time to send out an S.O.S.! Americans must once again find our anchor and repair our compass, so that we can chart a new course together. But we are running out of time, and we must act now!

As we strive to reestablish personal liberty and Constitutional governance throughout the land, we will continue to face tremendous obstacles and mounting pressures. Let us persevere to take back our nation with clarity of vision and the courage of true patriots.

> Hold on, my friends, to the Constitution and the Republic for which it stands. Miracles do not cluster, and what has happened once in 6,000 years, may not happen again. Hold on to the Constitution, for if the American Constitution should fail, there will be anarchy throughout the world. - Daniel Webster

# Chapter Four

# Citizens and Patriots

Citizenship and patriotism can be understood in many different ways. One of the chief aims of this book is to persuade you to believe that here in America these terms should be held dearly, close to the heart, and that we dare not take them lightly or else we may very well lose the freedoms for which our ancestors bled and died.

During the American Revolution, the colonists possessed a staunchly independent spirit. They were rugged individualists who knew the meaning of hard work, personal sacrifice and suffering. In that context, personal liberty was held in high regard and the spirit of resistance to tyranny found fertile ground.

In modern America, most of us have grown up in relatively comfortable surroundings, without much hardship or struggle in comparison to most of the world. We have taken for granted the many blessings that are ours, and over a period of time we have allowed ourselves to become both ignorant and complacent. As a whole, we have become detached and do not remember or appreciate our own history.

Recent generations have witnessed the gradual breakdown of morality within our society. Added financial pressures on families, the feminization of our culture and the confusion of gender roles have all contributed to the rapid disintegration of the family. Many who now reside in America are cultural foreigners; whether they are native born, legal immigrants or illegal aliens, they do not possess the true spirit of America. To be blunt, a huge majority of our people are now passive, lazy and stupid when it comes to understanding what it means to be a true American.

## Differing Views of the World

A 'worldview' is very simply the lens through which we see human history and society. It is the framework that establishes how we evaluate or interpret right and wrong, the events of history and the meaning or purpose of life itself. There are, of course, many different worldviews across the planet, all shaped by centuries of human tradition and experience. Our individual and corporate hopes and dreams revolve around our particular worldview.

For many around the globe, life is but an endless cycle of rebirth and death. Others view life mainly through family or cultural pride and traditions. Philosophy and religion also play a significant role in shaping the worldviews of people and cultures.

For some, worldview is not much more than a narrow experience of their own tribe or culture – one of self-promotion or preservation. Others societies have had the motivation and capability to extend their influence over others because their worldview included a broader scope.

Militant Islam is predicated on a worldview that is as old as time itself – one based on extreme prejudice, ethnic and religious superiority and a complete intolerance or acceptance of other views. Islam, by its very history, teachings and practices, is not a religion of peace, but rather one of exclusivity, domination and conquest. And this is carried out with barbarism and ruthless abandonment of human self-worth and dignity.

Socialism, fascism and communism are all ideologies that also represent particular worldviews. While promising equality for all and justice for the common man, in reality these systems actually deliver rule by an elite class. Injustice, a loss of personal liberty and responsibility and all incentives for excellence follow closely behind.

## The Other Manifestos

As I pondered writing a manifesto for American patriots, I often thought of the other manifestos that have come before – the Communist Manifesto, the Humanist Manifestos and even the Christian Manifesto, often quoted in this book. Each manifesto explains a different worldview; for example, the Communist Manifesto proposes:

1. Abolition of property in land and of all rents of land to public purposes.
2. A heavy progressive or graduated income tax.
3. Abolition of all right of inheritance.
4. Confiscation of the property of all emigrants and rebels.
5. Centralization of credit in the hands of the State, by means of a national bank with State capital and an exclusive monopoly.
6. Centralization of the means of communication and transport in the hands of the State.
7. Extension of factories and instruments of production owned by the State; the bringing into cultivation of waste-lands, and the improvement of the soil generally in accordance with a common plan.
8. Equal liability of all to labor. Establishment of industrial armies, especially for agriculture.
9. Combination of agriculture with manufacturing industries; gradual abolition of the distinction between town and country, by a more equitable distribution of the population over the country.

> 10. Free education for all children in public schools. Abolition of children's factory labor in its present form. Combination of education with industrial production.
>
> – The Ten Planks of the *Communist Manifesto*, Karl Marx and Friedrich Engels

The Humanist Manifestos reveal yet another worldview:

> Today man's larger understanding of the universe, his scientific achievements, and deeper appreciation of brotherhood, have created a situation which requires a new statement of the means and purposes of religion. Such a vital, fearless, and frank religion capable of furnishing adequate social goals and personal satisfactions may appear to many people as a complete break with the past. While this age does owe a vast debt to the traditional religions, it is none the less obvious that any religion that can hope to be a synthesizing and dynamic force for today must be shaped for the needs of this age. To establish such a religion is a major necessity of the present. It is a responsibility which rests upon this generation.
>
> - From the *Humanist Manifesto I*, 1933

> No deity will save us; we must save ourselves … We are responsible for what we are and for what we will be …
>
> - From the *Humanist Manifesto II*, 1973

Our struggle for liberty in the United States is all about worldviews that are diametrically opposed to one another. The primary conflict has become a classic struggle between the original Judeo-Christian worldview of Americans and that of secular humanism, which declares that truth and standards of morality are relative, and that man himself is the final authority.

> Nowhere have the divergent results of the two total concepts of reality, the Judeo-Christian and the humanist worldview, been more open to observation than in government and law... Humanism, with its lack of any final base for values and law, always leads to chaos. It then naturally leads to some form of authoritarianism to control the chaos. Having produced the sickness, humanism gives more of the same kind of medicine for a cure.
> – Francis Schaeffer, *A Christian Manifesto*

These manifestos represent a cosmic struggle for supremacy over the minds and hearts of human beings. Every system of belief, every proposed explanation and interpretation of man's history, social and psychological makeup all clamor to be heard and accepted. To this, I add my views and suggestions about a distinctly American point of view.

**An American Worldview**

Walt Whitman, famous American poet, once said, "No man's benefit should be achieved at the expense of his neighbors." This statement clearly reflects a basic American value – that we should be free to conduct our own personal lives as long as our actions do not infringe upon the rights of someone else. The role of government is not to regulate, enforce, provide for, ensure, or guarantee fairness or equal distribution, but to uphold the principles of personal responsibility, liberty, and the law.

America was founded upon a specific worldview. While acknowledging the existence and contributions of the various societies that have blended to form American culture, we must also recognize that our nation and our form of government were established on the foundation of a distinct Judeo-Christian worldview. Our nation was birthed and became great because of this foundation. Our Founding Fathers clearly acknowledged 'Divine Providence' or the guiding hand of God, throughout this process.

For those who might bristle in reaction to this idea, this does not imply that our Founding Fathers were trying to establish a particular religion or to exclude others. This statement is meant to reaffirm the basic moral code upon which our nation was founded - one that identified our societal standards of right and wrong. This formed the basis of our American culture and the bedrock for greatness. Whether you like it or not, the Founders clearly believed that the continuance of virtue was indispensable to the ongoing success of the republic.

> A general dissolution of principles and manners will more surely overthrow the liberties of America than the whole force of the common enemy. While the people are virtuous they cannot be subdued; but when once they lose their virtue they will be ready to surrender their liberties to the first external or internal invader.
> - Samuel Adams

## Establishing a Standard of Morality

It is frequently argued that we cannot 'legislate morality.' In favor of relaxing certain restraints, this argument ignores the fact that all laws designed to protect citizens from the harmful abuses of others are based on some form of a moral code. In other words, lying, cheating, stealing, adultery and murder are all clear examples of our societal system of morality.

A typical follow up argument is based on the reasoning that people should be free to do whatever they want if it does not personally injure someone else. This belief presupposes that we can somehow break the laws of God, as long as we do it privately, in the shadows or behind closed doors. The truth is that our character is inseparable from our conduct. Our choices and actions do affect others personally, as well as our society indirectly.

Both of these arguments become hollow when we consider that the ultimate issue is not about morality per se, but rather whose version of morality we will accept. We therefore are confronted with a choice between these opposing worldviews, and our decision will ultimately affect our future and that of our nation.

**Reshaping the Image of Patriotism**

I am a firm believer in looking in the mirror first before criticizing others. One of our first steps should be to reexamine what we believe about patriotism. Often misunderstood or shrouded in an ambiguous cloud, the term 'patriot' is rarely understood correctly. Those in power often misinterpret the meaning deliberately in order to discredit others who do not support their agendas.

For many Americans, the word patriot conjures up mixed feelings. On one hand, we instinctively know that being a patriot is right and honorable, yet we are also confused by cultural changes and the misuse of this term. What few of us realize is that behind the scenes there is a deliberate effort to reshape the thinking of the American people. This is directly correlated with declining cultural and educational trends, coupled with a rapid increase in the number of immigrants who are not fully assimilating into our American language and culture. As we pursue multicultural acceptance and a global community, we do so at the peril of losing our own identity and national sovereignty.

**Patriotism Today**

Allow me to paint a picture of many modern American 'patriots.' For many, patriotism involves occasional warm, fuzzy feelings of affection for our nation. We wave flags, remember holidays and appreciate our veterans, or make use of slogans like 'God bless America' or 'support our troops.' This form of patriotism, while nice, is not deeply rooted in our hearts and minds. It is not based on a clear understanding of our unique history or the principles of liberty upon which our nation was founded. As a result, it is shallow at best, and will shift with the wind or wilt under any form of pressure.

A growing number of Americans, who have long been asleep, are now awakening to what is happening in our country. Many of these people are stirred up, even angry, yet they still do not have a firm grasp of our history, the Constitution, or the basic principles of liberty. Because they also do not know what has happened in the patriot community over the past 20 or 30 years, they naively gravitate towards political activism, as they perceive this to be the best way to get involved. This response represents a rather uninformed or shallow approach to a deep national crisis.

At this point in time, it is sheer insanity to busy ourselves with attempts to elect new politicians, who would supposedly reverse the trends of a thoroughly inept, corrupt and broken political system. According to the often-repeated modern definition of insanity, how can we expect different results while clinging on to the same worn out ideas and practices?

> Freedom means not only that our economic activity ought to be free and voluntary, but that

> our government should stay out of our personal affairs as well… The war on terror has awakened more Americans than ever to the way government exploits fear, and even its own failures, to justify eroding our civil liberties.
> – Ron Paul, *The Revolution: A Manifesto*

Working through the existing political or legal channels has produced a few minor victories; but overall these efforts have been ineffectual in turning the overwhelming tide. This should be obvious by now. Complaining or rehashing what we already know will not save our Republic either. Time is not on our side at this point! We must now face these realities and forge ahead together with fresh, new ideas and plans.

By way of contrast, true patriots are those who love their country, deeply and passionately. They are persons who understand our history and embrace fundamental American values; someone who will take a stand against all enemies who would threaten to take away what they have come to hold so dearly; a person who will not compromise or surrender. The true patriot will arise in a time of crisis to defend liberty and die if necessary to preserve our nation for future generations.

**Keyboard Commandos**

We sometimes use the phrase 'backseat driver' to identify someone who tries to offer driving tips while riding as a passenger. Similarly, we also use the term 'armchair quarterback' to refer to people who, from a comfortable vantage point, seem to have all the right ideas. Within the patriot community, the growing trend in our internet-laden world is for people to become bogged down or entrenched at their computer keyboards. These pseudo-patriots, often well meaning and sincere, spend countless hours surfing the web, composing or forwarding massive amounts of email. Yet many of them seem reluctant to come out of their computerized caves. Their frequent lack of people skills and direct involvement has been a real hindrance to the growth of the patriot movement in America.

My experience has been that far too often these 'keyboard commandos' do not seem to have time to engage people in the real world. They are slow to volunteer for real work or tasks, and like much of our present generation, are often not diligent or dependable when they do volunteer. As someone who witnesses this frequently, I think I can safely say that thousands of patriots live inside boxes that are clogged with conspiracy theories, trivial data and re-circulated information. If even a portion of the vast amounts of time and energy spent on the internet would be invested in real community and political activism, think how much further along our cause would be.

**Overcoming Ignorance and Apathy**

The restoration of America is inextricably linked to the awakening and mobilization of the American people. Until we gain the informed support of the people and arouse the absolute dedication of a relentless band of patriots, we will not witness a real breakthrough.

In my first book, *The Downward Spiral: Decline of the American Dream*, I hammered hard on the curse of apathy that has engulfed our nation. Since that time, I am happy to report that many Americans have begun to wake up and seriously consider the plight of our Republic. Still, whether or not this awakening is enough to turn the tide is yet to be determined.

> A nation of well informed men who have been taught to know and prize the rights which God has given them cannot be enslaved. It is in the region of ignorance that tyranny begins.
> - Benjamin Franklin

In America, citizenship should involve an active role in the process of government. To be a good citizen means that you do not sit back and allow others to make decisions or run the show. You must involve yourself in the process by being educated, active and vigilant.

**The Challenge Before Us**

If ever the patriot movement needs to look in the mirror and wake up, that time is most certainly now! We cannot expect the masses of unlearned, disconnected Americans to suddenly realize what is going on, if we do not accept the responsibility of engaging them on a personal level. Unless we assume the roles of educators and motivators, our fellow citizens will continue to believe whatever is spoon-fed to them by the media and our politicians.

With over half of the voting population either not voting, or already accepting socialistic and humanistic values, we now face the formidable task of educating our fellow Americans – the multitudes who have wandered away from our American heritage and form of government. They now outnumber us by far, and if we do not rise to this challenge soon, they will seek to completely disregard, and eventually destroy us. This is because we stand in the way of the transformation that they are bringing upon our nation.

# Chapter Five

# Dreaming of a New America

Call it a dream ... or nostalgia ... or pure idealism – I just can't help it. I keep dreaming of an America where people are once again truly free. A country where people experience the type of liberty that our Founding Fathers envisioned. A place where people get to keep their hard-earned money. Where they are responsible for themselves and look out for their fellow citizens.

Historically, America has been a haven for immigrants and refuges from around the globe. Here they have found unsurpassed freedom and opportunity. Yet today, many immigrants come, not to become true Americans, but rather because they can tap into our system without sacrifice or hard work; without embracing our language, culture, or American values.

Perhaps even worse, many Americans themselves have lost sight of these same core values.

**Days Gone By**

I can still remember when it was safe for children to play outside or run around the neighborhood. They got plenty of exercise and for the most part excelled in school and in life. Their families were generally healthy and intact. Fathers and mothers had distinct and equally important roles to play in the family. Our neighborhoods were friendlier places then and our communities were much safer.

I remember days gone by, when education, politics and the economy were not so constantly focused on money or divvying up the pie of government funding. A time when people believed that hard work was the way to success and prosperity. They did not expect the government to take care of them, or for others to pay their way.

I remember the days when the daily news was not filled with the faces of criminals – drunks, robbers, murderers, rapists and child molesters. This constant flood of inconceivable, disgusting acts by the low life of our society is not news, but rather a nagging reminder of the condition of our nation. On top of this, the frequent scandals of celebrities, community leaders and politicians have become so commonplace that we have grown accustomed to these atrocities.

I still remember … don't you? Perhaps this America will never be seen again. I don't know for sure. But I long for it anyway.

**Restoring Virtue and Character**

Heroes and role models who are decent, upstanding citizens are becoming increasingly hard to find. Even when we think we have found one, they frequently stumble and are exposed for some disgraceful behavior.

While contemplating the restoration of America, I cling to the unpopular and politically incorrect opinion that virtue and character must once again become so prevalent in our society that these evils will no longer be tolerated. In other words, the light of good behavior must shine into every corner and illuminate our path, while at the same time exposing those whose deeds are a blight on our communities and our nation.

Personal freedom and responsibility form the bedrock of our Republic. These two balance one another. Personal responsibility is the missing link in our society, and because we are in such short supply, we have need of more government control and regulation. Is this what you want? If we will not govern ourselves, or if we have no conscience or clear standards of right and wrong, what else can we expect?

Upholding, yes, even demanding higher standards is essential to restoring true liberty and America's greatness. Our Founding Fathers rightly understood that virtue was indispensable to maintaining our form of government.

**Leading the World**

I dream of an America that truly leads the world again – by example, by innovation, by strength of conviction and character.

The United States grew to world power status by leading the way in these areas. Along the way, we made friends and allies, built bridges of cooperation and became an example of productivity, fairness and justice. We will not retain this stature by succumbing to the tactics and practices of evil men, dictators or third world governments.

We need to police ourselves, not the rest of the world. Others will once again admire us and want what we have if we will once again behave like true Americans! In the absence of true character, we have no recourse but to resort to political and economic coercion, manipulation, bribery and under the table deals. The use of unethical practice or force is always a sign of cultural deterioration.

America has long been a leader in compassion and global humanitarian aid. Helping the poor and needy is a natural act for those who are generous in spirit. Americans leads the way in demonstrating compassion when people across the globe suffer from natural or man-made disasters. This does not need to be mandated through taxation, government control or regulation. It is a matter of the heart. When people are free and virtuous, they will help others voluntarily.

**What Are We Fighting For?**

I think you too may remember when America went to war decisively, under Constitutional authority, and then actually defeated our enemies. It has been a long time, but those wars were justified and truly fought to preserve our freedom. Our international posture was primarily defensive and we did not arrogantly assume to be the policeman of the entire planet.

In contrast, we now station our troops around the globe and meddle in the affairs of other nations. We now become embedded in seemingly endless wars, against foes that are far inferior; and we have no clear purpose or deep commitment to win. This is because we are now manipulated by the hidden agendas and ulterior motives of those who are in power or hold the purse strings.

In order to 'make America safe,' we now penalize and punish our own citizens, gradually stripping them of the very rights we claim to protect. While maintaining an illusion of focusing on criminals, terrorists and foreign enemies, we place a heavier yoke of financial burden and tyranny upon our own people.

**Real Leaders**

I dream of American leaders who are genuine examples to the people – leaders who sacrifice, inspire and motivate us to live a better way – the American way. Is this not possible? Can we not find leaders that we can trust; whose character and selfless behavior makes us want to follow them? Do we really have to accept and tolerate these sub-American standards and this endless cycle of dishonesty and doubletalk?

I might be crazy, but still I ponder the possibilities of elected officials who are true statesmen, not career politicians who live in such an incubated environment that they become detached from the people and thoroughly corrupt. In my imagined world, instead of abusing their power and extracting their livelihood from the people, they would actually live on our level, as part of our communities. They would truly represent us. And when their brief time of government service was completed, they would return home to be a productive part of our society once again.

**It All Starts at Home**

My dream takes me back to a place where people understand and embrace personal responsibility. Instead of blaming others, acting like victims or beggars, people would actually assume full responsibility for their own lives and future. They would not seek or even expect handouts, welfare and short cuts.

In this renewed America, the law would be clear and simple. You break the law – you suffer the consequences – period. We would live in a society that was not driven by monetary gain, but by the principles of fairness and justice. There would be no more judicial maze, frivolous lawsuits, plea bargains and subjective, constantly changing interpretations of the law.

**Finding our Future in the Past**

Sometimes the best path to take is an old one. We can learn from history and our own mistakes, if we would collectively have a change of heart.

And so the call goes out, to all who will hear:

> Stand at the crossroads and look; ask for the ancient paths, ask where the good way is, and walk in it, and you shall find rest for your souls.
> – Jeremiah 6:16, New International Version

**The Dream Lives On**

And so I dream on, of an America where the people are free to innovate, work diligently and keep the fruit of their hard-earned labor. A nation where hard work, creativity and innovation are rewarded and not discouraged or punished by greater taxation and the redistribution of wealth.

The heartbeat of true American patriots today is to bring back this dream. The only way to do so is to restore these values and Constitutional governance in our nation. I sincerely hope that we have the needed resolve and time to do so.

# Chapter Six

# Finding Common Ground

America today is facing challenges that threaten our stability, prosperity and future as a nation. Simultaneously, from many different directions, we are being confronted with massive, mind-boggling spending, debt and internal turmoil. This type of 'change' is catapulting us toward socialism, globalism and disaster at a reckless speed.

Are the problems we face as a nation merely circumstantial, or part of a normal economic or political cycle? Our leaders claim to be experts and the best ones to guide us out of this mess. Are we to believe that they are sincere and truly unaware of what is going on? Is the answer to out-of-control spending and debt really more spending and bigger government? Should we place our trust in those who have actually created the predicament in which we now find ourselves? I wonder if there just might be another, more plausible explanation.

**We Are on a Collision Course**

The sooner we accept and embrace the sobering reality that America is on a collision course, the better off we will be. This collision course is being caused by those who are intent on transforming our nation into something far different from the vision of our Founding Fathers. This is no less than a deliberate, even diabolical strategy to guide our nation into the chains of tyranny and an all-powerful government. There is a deep rift between the opposing worldviews and values of many Americans, and by abandoning the vision and principles of our Founding Fathers, our government is forcing a confrontation.

We are living in tumultuous times – ignoring this or wishing it would just go away will only ensure our progressive enslavement to tyranny. Many independent financial experts are sounding the alarm, warning of the imminent and total financial collapse of our economy. Every week legislation is considered or passed that continues to shred the Constitution, erode our liberties and pave the way for a more pervasive, controlling government. The amount of money they flippantly discuss is staggering, and the deceptive concealment of the true problems and motives is alarming, to say the least.

Fortunately, the people and the States are beginning to speak out and fight back. Through activism, legislation and protest, the voice of the people is beginning to rise. With the help of Almighty God, the people are, in reality, our best hope for survival and the restoration of our Republic. Yet they must be awakened – in mass. And they must be equipped, organized and deeply committed to the cause of liberty in order for us to achieve victory.

Perhaps the light at the end of the tunnel is that recent events are finally beginning to wake up the American people! The emergence of the Tea Party movement and many other patriotic groups across the United States clearly reveals the mounting frustration and ire of the people. All over this great land, millions of freedom-loving patriots are not only stirring, but also beginning to mobilize for action and real change.

## Not a Partisan Issue

While the number of Americans waking up is increasing, many naively believe that the troubles facing our nation are still an issue between the two major political parties. The rally cry and efforts to revitalize the Republican Party fail to recognize the corruption and political machinery that has become the trademark of both parties for a long time. Rather than focusing on bashing the Democrats and returning Republicans to power, people should examine history and the real issues more deeply. Upon doing so, the stark realization would soon come that neither Democrats nor Republicans have the answers that America needs. No, this is not a partisan issue – the only thing at stake with the two parties is the speed at which we fly off the cliff into destruction.

### A Serious Dilemma Within the Patriot Movement

With the best of intentions, many individuals and groups within the patriot movement spend countless time, energy and money struggling to achieve the most minor of victories, usually on one isolated battlefront. Here's a newsflash, folks: we are losing the war! It should be quite obvious by now that these efforts have neither turned the tide, nor abated the relentless push toward globalism and tyranny by the world bankers and our own government. Our own disunity is our biggest problem.

> Numerous groups are working hard to restore Constitutional principles in our nation, yet there is not an overall unity or a cohesive strategy between them. Most are focused on a particular issue, such as abortion, illegal immigration, property rights, taxes, etc. Unfortunately, this often becomes a never-ending battle to put out individual wildfires, and without a coordinated effort to wake up the American people this will not be enough to stop the raging forest fire that threatens to engulf our entire nation.
> - Dave Batcheller, *The Downward Spiral: Decline of the American Dream*

> We are all fighting a war on many fronts, which has effectively divided our troops and resources. This is why we have been so easy to defeat. If we

> can pool our resources and agree to fight this cultural war on one front, and focus our energies on one specific objective, we can be unstoppable.
> – John Diamond, *The Rise of America*

Perhaps when sufficient numbers of leaders from these various groups wake up and face the reality of the impending crisis in our nation, we will then witness the emergence of true patriot leadership and the rallying of the American people for the cause of liberty once again. Thus far, we have only repeated a sad history of allowing our narrow vision, egos and personal agendas to cause further splintering and disunity.

**What Can We Do?**

Even the average person on the street senses that something is seriously wrong in our country. Yet the paralyzing grip caused by ignorance, apathy and helplessness still needs to be broken. Apparently, for many of us, only dire consequences or severe testing at a personal level will break this grip. For the millions of us who are starting to wake up, we must quickly learn both the principles of liberty and then how to work together, focusing our energies on the most critical areas.

The American people must begin to believe again that each person's voice and effort does matter, and that they can together affect the change that is so desperately needed. We must revive hope and stir the patriotic passions of the American people. These tyrants and idiots must be held accountable for their actions!

We must bridge the gaps that separate and divide us, whether it is our age, race, religious views, ideologies or values. Historically, this has been the enduring quality of the American spirit and we must once again shake off negativity and indifference and rise to this challenge.

> Educate and inform the whole mass of the people … They are the only sure reliance for the preservation of our liberty.
> – Thomas Jefferson

**We Must Find and Focus on Our Rally Point**

In the heat of battle, facing imminent threat and danger, soldiers are trained to regroup at a pre-designated rally point. There they can reorganize and plan their counter attack on the enemy.

For years, the patriot movement has allowed itself to be splintered or divided into a multitude of issue-oriented groups, all attempting to put out the wildfires of causes that they are passionate about. As important as these issues are, we must now find our common ground as fellow American patriots. This rally point is undoubtedly the foundational principles of our Founding Fathers, embodied in the Declaration of Independence, the United States Constitution and the Bill of Rights. We may not agree on many other things, but on these points we must be firmly united! My experience has taught me that nearly everyone within our movement is agreed on these core values; and that beyond this point we begin to disagree on numerous issues. Clearly, these core values can unite us!

It is fine for us to continue our struggles with all these individual causes. Yet it is time, I believe, for us to see the bigger picture, uniting together at this rally point. We can then work as one in a spirit of cooperation and gain the added strength and synergy of the mass movement that is needed to bring tyranny to its knees.

Rallying in this way will require us to refocus and prioritize, perhaps even to lay aside our narrow agendas, pet projects and egos. If we do not, the risk of losing everything, including our Constitutional Republic, is very real!

**The Time is Upon Us**

Now is the time for true patriots and leaders to step forward. There is no time for endless rehashing of the causes or problems. We must shift our focus to action and resistance! As a unified force, we must now begin the arduous task of taking back our country from the most powerful and deceptively corrupt government on the face of the planet.

With a deep commitment to the principles of liberty, and with the fiery passion of true patriots, we must now draw the line and refuse to remain silent or compliant. We may have already allowed things to go too far, but of this we must be certain - we cannot and will not allow the insane actions of our politicians to run their course and destroy America.

Will you stand up now? Will you unite around these core values and rise up together for freedom and the American dream? My hope and prayer is that today you will hear the call and not turn back.

# Chapter Seven

# Overcoming the Obstacles

Restoring the American Republic will be an arduous task at best. There are so many complex issues and obstacles to overcome that many people have already become disheartened or pessimistic. At the very outset, we need to review the true purpose of government.

> First, we need to rethink what the role of government ought to be, and fast. If we continue to think of our government as the policeman of the world and as the Great Provider from cradle to grave, our problems will grow worse and our downward economic spiral, the first signs of which we are now witnessing, will only accelerate.
> – Ron Paul, *The Revolution: A Manifesto*

Once we have established the legitimate purpose of government - to uphold the Constitution and protect the rights of its citizens - we can then begin to consider how to overcome the following hurdles.

**Corporate Clout – Money Talks**

The first obstacle we must somehow overcome is that of corporate interests. By allowing our politicians to be adversely influenced and bought off by large corporations, we yield our principles to the almighty dollar. Backroom deals and favors granted to corporate entities must not be allowed if we wish to preserve our Republic.

**Special Interest Groups – Control by the Minority**

The erosion caused by catering to special interest groups is very similar. In this case, we surrender the principles of liberty to the squeakiest wheel, most often a small minority of people who have the backing of huge funding sources and the media. It is unbelievable that the will of the people is so frequently circumvented through this process. Again, we must put an end to this!

**Elections – The Ultimate Smoke Screen**

The 'appearance of democracy' is maintained by those in power primarily through the ultimate smoke screen of the election process. Here again, money is often the determining factor in who is able to mount a serious campaign. We desperately need radical election reform, which would break the stranglehold that inhibits legitimate candidates, third parties and independents from delivering their messages to the American people. Of course, passing legislation that would mandate campaign finance reform or term limits is desperately needed too, yet virtually impossible at present, since it has to be voted on by the very people who hold the reins of power.

**The Media Filter**

Everyone seems to acknowledge the slanted, biased influence of the media, yet like these other obstacles, no one can figure out a way to resolve the predicament. The media is simply the mouthpiece of the same corporations and special interest groups that are bent on reshaping America. Until the people themselves become both educated and outspoken enough to expose and counteract the media propaganda with the truth, there will be little hope for a true national restoration.

**When Government Fails**

Our Founding Fathers deeply understood the influence and corruption associated with greed and monetary control. One of their battle cries was 'taxation without representation,' which today could be reinterpreted as 'representation without restraint.' We are reminded frequently that the vast majority of Americans do not approve of Congress or the White House, yet nothing changes. The ebb and flow of election cycles does little more than a changing of the guard – nothing else changes. We seem to be caught in an endless cycle, enslaved to those who rule over us.

The American government has clearly failed to perform its most basic function, while daily involving itself in matters not authorized by the United States Constitution. These violations are both serious and treasonous offenses against the American people! The response of our leaders, thus far, has been to completely ignore our petitions and appeals. While doing so, they actually have the gall to deride our Founding Fathers, if not openly, then for sure by their actions.

> If our critics want to repudiate the Founding Fathers, let them go ahead and do it. If they won't be honest enough to do so, they should at least refrain from condemning those of us who still believe in the wisdom they left for posterity.
> – Ron Paul, *The Revolution: A Manifesto*

When all three branches of government are guilty of collusion to abandon the vision of our Founding Fathers, it falls upon the people themselves to rectify the crisis. The Declaration of Independence acknowledges our authority to do so. The fortress created by this intricate web of obstacles can and will be broken by the determined, unified voice of a people who still believe in our Constitutional Republic. Our leaders seem to believe that they are above the law and can do whatever they want. This all is about to change!

## When Good People Sleep

The heartland of America is filled with people who are decent, law-abiding citizens. They share a common language and work ethic. They believe in God and in America. They have traditional or conservative values. Yet for years, this huge block of American voters has been sidelined or neutralized through devious tactics and deceptive messages.

The American church alone represents a force that could easily turn things around in our nation. Yet America's pastors and church members, for the most part, have been taken out of the game. Most actually believe that they are not even supposed to be in the political arena. And while they have been asleep, America has been taken over.

> Despite the differences, the American church, like that of Nazi Germany, is in danger of wrapping the cross of Christ in some alien flag.
> – Erwin Lutzer, *Hitler's Cross*

## Unraveling the Lies and Deception

For many Americans, protest and civil disobedience are concepts that are both misunderstood and undesirable. Having lived for so long in relative peace or tranquility, sheltered from the effects of personal discrimination or suffering, most of us have allowed ourselves to become complacent. As decent human beings, we generally respect others and just want to be left alone. The very thought of becoming a radical and standing up for what is right seems distasteful or unnecessary to us. Yet our opponents do not play by the same rules.

At the crux of these paralyzing lies, there is a direct manipulation of the facts. It seems that we have been bound by certain teachings that cause us remain disconnected and uninvolved. These deceptive teachings, while sounding correct or even honorable on the surface, lead us down a path that makes us vulnerable to those who would take advantage of us and pervert the very foundations of liberty established here in America.

**Loyalty to Caesar or to God?**

Some of the obstacles we must overcome are less outward, but represent more of an ideological battle. One of the most hideous lies thrust upon the American people is that 'religion and politics do not mix,' falsely interpreted to mean that people of faith should not be involved with social issues or politics. The result has been that good people have not been involved and therefore evil and corruption have run rampant throughout our culture.

The Bible records an interesting story about a time when Jesus was challenged by the religious leaders of his day, who attempted to set an inescapable trap for him. We read this story in Mark 12:13-17:

> And they sent some of the Pharisees and Herodians to him, in order to trap him in a statement. And they came and said to him, "Teacher, we know that you are truthful, and defer to no one; for you are not partial to any, but teach the way of God in truth. Is it lawful to pay a poll tax to Caesar, or not? Shall we pay, or shall we not pay?" But he, knowing their hypocrisy, said to them, "Why are you testing me? Bring me a denarius to look at." And they brought one, and he said to them, "Whose likeness and inscription is this?" And they said to him, "Caesar's." And

> Jesus said to them, "Render to Caesar the things that are Caesar's, and to God the things that are God's." And they were amazed at him.

This passage of scripture has been interpreted in different ways over the years, usually incorrectly. Consider the following thoughts concerning Jesus' answer to this question:

> Here Jesus is addressing his enemies – or rather the *agent's provocateurs* whom they had sent – while attempting to wiggle out of an elaborate trap by which they hoped to ensnare and eventually destroy him. As he was wont to do in such situations, the Lord did not dignify an essentially dishonest question with a straightforward answer. Instead, his response is elliptical almost to the point of being evasive; when the occasion called for it, Jesus could follow his own advice to the disciples to be wise as serpents and innocent as doves…
>
> This text has often been used to support the thoroughly unchristian notion that political matters are of no concern to God, and its corollary, that they need not be of any concern to us. – Michael Cromartie, *Caesar's Coin Revisited*

Controversy and disgruntled feelings about paying taxes to government have been around throughout history. It is no doubt, a natural condition of the world in which we live, that rulers would devise ways to oppress and extract the livelihood of others for their own benefit. However, was Jesus' response, as some suggest, merely an affirmation of our obligation to submit or obey those who govern over us? I think not. Cromartie goes on to identify a dual purpose in the response of Christ:

> How does all this help to illuminate the meaning of Jesus' rather cryptic answer? My contention is that it suggests a twofold purpose: to negate Caesar's claim to absolute authority, not to mention divinity, and to undercut the essentially anarchist logic of the Zealots' argument that since God has exclusive rights over his people, the claims of human government are illegitimate.
> – Michael Cromartie, *Caesar's Coin Revisited*

The response of Jesus clearly indicates that we should acknowledge a higher authority than that of human government. At the same time, he does not negate our responsibility to honor or obey our rulers when they are operating as servants and administrators of justice for society. The example from this story should guide us as we seek to find the proper balance in complicated or controversial issues.

For many Americans, the real issue at stake here is to not allow the edicts of government to overshadow our personal conscience or the higher laws of God. When government fails to uphold what is right and allows itself to become corrupt and evil, we are no longer under an obligation to submit to its authority.

**Ultimate Submission**

In the same way, millions of otherwise patriotic Americans have been duped into believing that we must submit to any governmental authority that is over us. The culprits that proclaim this message are often the pastors of America. Romans 13:1-7 is often cited to suggest that submission to governmental authority is always binding and unconditional.

> Let every person be in subjection to the governing authorities, for there is no authority except from God, and those which exist are

> established by God. Therefore he who resists authority has opposed the ordinance of God; and they who have opposed will receive condemnation upon themselves. For rulers are not a cause of fear for good behavior, but for evil. Do you want to have no fear of authority? Do what is good, and you will have praise from the same; for it is a minister of God to you for good. But if you do what is evil, be afraid; for it does not bear the sword for nothing; for it is a minister of God, an avenger who brings wrath upon the one who practices evil. Wherefore it is necessary to be in subjection, not only because of wrath, but also for conscience' sake. For because of this you pay taxes, for rulers are servants of God, devoting themselves to this very thing. Render to all what is due them; tax to whom tax is due; custom to whom custom; fear to who fear; honor to whom honor (emphasis by the author).

It is clear from this passage that rulers are assumed to be the agents of justice, representatives of divine authority. Their primary responsibility is to protect citizens from the evil deeds of their peers, not to restrict or punish those who are good. In referring to the above passage in the Bible, Francis Schaeffer made this astute observation:

> God has ordained the state as a delegated authority; it is not autonomous. The state is to be an agent of justice, to restrain evil by punishing the wrongdoer, and to protect the good in society. When it does the reverse, it has no proper authority. It is then a usurped authority and as such it becomes lawless and is tyranny.
> – Francis Schaeffer, *A Christian Manifesto*

Both of these common misinterpretations are lies that demonstrate inconsistent and faulty reasoning. While most Americans pay tribute to our veterans and believe that it is honorable to die for one's country in a land far away, most will not resist evil or tyranny here at home. We embrace the idea of fighting the enemies of freedom or democracy in just wars; yet somehow we do not believe that we have the same fundamental rights on a personal basis. Do we not have a personal right to freedom, self-government and self-defense? Or at what point do we draw the line when those in power are the ones acting immorally or illegally? How much will we allow the government to abuse and tax us before they own us completely, like serfs or slaves?

After swallowing these lies, many people view government as being on a pedestal higher than personal liberty. This is not only very wrong, but also backwards thinking! Even though we are aware of the frequent, glaring violations of law and human rights by our own government, why do we still choose to look the other way? Who will punish evil when it is the government doing it?

Are we supposed to believe that being quietly submissive is more honorable or pure? Even though we verbally honor our Founding Fathers, would they have tolerated this type of tyranny and abuse? The answer is that they resisted tyranny at all costs, first through the appeal process, then through civil disobedience and ultimately by shedding their blood. The pastors at that time were not part of the problem, as they are today, but rather an active part of the solution, many speaking out, and some even taking up arms when they had to.

## Adjusting Our Thinking

Most Americans still believe that dictators like Hitler or Mao were evil, that Communism is wrong, or that radical Islam is our enemy; yet often these beliefs are disconnected from our daily lives. This leads to deception, hypocrisy and half-hearted patriotism. Government is not exempt from following the law or upholding their oath to the Constitution. When they violate the higher laws of God or our own Constitution, they are subject to being brought back in line, either by the people themselves, by the consequences of a national crisis, or by defeat at the hand of our enemies. At this point, we can only hope that the people will save us from our government!

> The term government does not, therefore, imply any particular form of society of any particular form of state. Government is divinely ordained authority to exercise worldly dominion by divine right. Government is deputyship for God on earth…
>
> … {the individual's} duty of obedience is binding… until government directly compels him to offend against the divine commandment, that it to say, until government openly denies its divine commission and thereby forfeits its claims. In cases of doubt, obedience is required; for the Christian does not bear the responsibility of the government. But if government violates or exceeds its commission at any point, for example by making itself master over the behalf of the congregation, then at this point, indeed, obedience is to be refused, for conscience' sake, for the Lord's sake. – Dietrich Bonhoeffer, *Ethics*
>
> Christians have political attachments to be sure, and they must take their civic responsibilities seriously; but they can never confuse the claims of Caesar with the higher claims of God.
> – Michael Cromartie, *Caesar's Coin Revisited*

## What are a Free People to Do?

While many cling to the fleeting hopes that they can bring reform through political channels, others are beginning to realize that we have in fact moved beyond the appeal process. For many years, liberty-minded Americans have questioned and challenged the policies and legislation of those who seek to undermine our Constitutional Republic. This battle has been fought on many fronts. Appeals, motions and legal proceedings have been filed, yet to no avail. The government has repeatedly turned a deaf ear and refused to answer our requests. In fact, the violations have increased substantially over the past few years. If we are to remain a truly free people, then what can we do at this point? Here are some of my observations regarding our best options.

## The Reassertion of States' Rights

A movement has been growing over the past several years for States to exert their rights under the 10th Amendment to the U.S. Constitution, which states:

> The powers not delegated to the United States by the Constitution, nor prohibited by it to the States, are reserved to the States respectively, or to the people.

As the federal government continues to expand its powers, through monetary bailouts and government controlled healthcare, the national rift grows deeper. With anger and tensions mounting, most states are still not complying with the Real ID law passed in 2005. Lawmakers in over forty states have introduced measures that warn Congress not to trample states' rights any further. At least seven of those states have actually passed such legislation.

Other measures opposing the federal government have been introduced, specifically dealing with issues like health care, immigration and gun control. In the days to come, this approach will undoubtedly be a way to ratchet up the defiance and send a clear message to the federal government.

## The Power of the Purse and the Sword

Dr. Edwin Vieira Jr., a constitutional attorney and scholar, has for years researched these issues and challenged the government at many points. He has concluded that our struggle boils down to two primary elements, what he calls the 'power of the purse' and 'the power of the sword.' His contention is that government holds its power based on these two essentials – the control of money and the control of military strength. In other words, by controlling our money system and having the biggest guns, the government can easily manipulate everything else. Our response must therefore include restoring a sound monetary system and providing a deterrent to the ever-expanding police state here in America.

## Restoring a Sound Money Policy

For some time, America's financial system has undergone a gradual transformation, which has taken us off a gold or silver standard and catapulted us into a system of fiat currency. This may very well become our undoing as a nation.

> Throughout most of American history, the dollar has been defined as a specific weight in gold. Until 1933, in fact, 20 dollars could be redeemed for one ounce of gold. But that year, the U.S. government went off the gold standard, and henceforth American currency would be redeemable into nothing. The government

> actually confiscated Americans' holdings of monetary gold.
> – Ron Paul, *The Revolution: A Manifesto*

A growing number of Americans are becoming aware of the deception that revolves around the Federal Reserve Bank. Continuing to expose this fraud, and pushing for a return to a constitutional, sound money system, is another important way that we can take back our Republic. Dissolving the Federal Reserve and returning our monetary control to Congress, as dictated by constitutional mandate, must be accomplished soon if we are to avert a national disaster.

> All the perplexities, confusions, and distress in America, arise, not from defects in their Constitution or Confederation, not from a want of honor or virtue, so much as from downright ignorance of the nature of coin, credit, and circulation. – President John Adams

> It's time for some fresh thinking for a change – an unbiased, rational reappraisal of a monetary system that is presented to us as the best of all possible worlds, but whose dangers grow clearer and more urgent with each passing day.
> – Ron Paul, *The Revolution: A Manifesto*

**Revitalizing the Constitutional Militias**

In the minds of our Founding Fathers, an armed population was the ultimate safeguard against tyranny. If all else failed, the people would still be able to defend themselves. Throughout history, when populations have been disarmed, there has been an unabated rush toward complete government domination.

In the early days of our Republic, all men between the ages of 18 and 45 were considered part of the militia - a community based self-defense force. This civilian force was trained and kept ready for community protection and as a deterrent against outside oppression or attack.

The concept of citizen militias, which has evolved over the years, has also become the subject of much debate. Once again, government and the media have utilized propaganda tactics to paint a negative picture. And it does not help that there are always be a few individuals whose extreme views or actions taint our movement. There is no question, however, that the people have the inherent right, not only to personal self-defense, but also to band together as free men in defense of their homes, communities and shared values. The Constitution and the Second Amendment in particular, upholds these rights, stating that:

> A well regulated Militia, being necessary to the security of a Free State, the right of the people to keep and bear arms, shall not be infringed.

The revitalization of the constitutional militias is an important and necessary part of maintaining our liberties here in America. At the same time, it is imperative, especially at this crucial point in time, that we do this in a sane, balanced way. Any law or practice, which inhibits these rights, or places control of all law enforcement or military under the exclusive control of the government, is a direct infringement of this right.

We must work hard to avoid the mistakes and stigmas attached to previous militia movements, if we are to be successful in restoring our nation. While acknowledging both the existence of a radical fringe of extremists, as well as government propaganda tactics, we must steer a straight course by not associating with these extremists or allowing ourselves to be lumped together with them. We need to learn how to fight back against the propaganda, for certainly the government does not back off when one of their own is caught or goes overboard. No, they make excuses, cover up, distance themselves and then move forward when the smoke clears. We must take a higher road, yet still expose the misinformation by shining the light of the truth.

## Enforcing the Law

Another growing movement in the United States seeks to uphold the authority of our county sheriffs as another deterrent to federal usurpation. Since the county sheriff has the ultimate authority to resist or stop all federal agencies within their jurisdiction, this becomes another clear line of defense.

The sheriff is an elected official, not a bureaucratic employee. They possess the ultimate law enforcement authority in their county. The county sheriff has taken an oath, like our other officials, to uphold and defend the Constitution of the United States. We may therefore approach them, both in respect for their office, as well as to solicit their support in turning back and even prosecuting those who operate unconstitutionally. This is now beginning to take place in counties all over the nation.

There is however, a move in our country to undermine the authority of county sheriffs by congressional authority and by implementing unconstitutional provisions of the Patriot Act. This had led some to conclude that the County Sheriff is our last hope or line of defense in America. Again, we must be aware of the enemy's tactics.

## Reviving the Citizen Grand Juries

Originating in the Magna Carta, the citizen's grand jury, also know as the people's panel, was an institution brought from England to the American colonies. Grand juries provided a means for citizens to protect themselves from abuses by the king and his agents.

The U.S. Constitution mentions the grand jury in Article Five of the Bill of Rights:

> No person shall be held to answer for a capital or otherwise infamous crime, unless on a presentment or indictment of a Grand Jury …

The grand jury is actually an independent institution adopted by our Founding Fathers to protect the individual from prosecutorial misconduct. It was pre-constitutional in origin, and from 1789 when the Bill of Rights was ratified, until the codification of the Federal Rules of Criminal Procedure in 1946, the grand jury was not regulated by statute. Of course, all three branches of government have shared a common interest in limiting the power of the citizen grand jury – and consistent with the decline of our nation, they have been seriously eroded over the past couple of generations.

Reviving the citizen grand juries will be another vital step in our stand against the systematic takeover of our Constitutional form of government.

**A Leadership Vacuum**

As I travel and interact with people across New Mexico and the nation, I have found a desperate need within the patriot movement – a vacuum of leadership. Sure, we have plenty of talking heads and leaders who are too full of themselves. Some of our mouthpieces seem to only scare people to death or make them angry. Most simply lack the character qualities of true leaders or they fail to see the big picture.

I see this tremendous shortage of solid, capable leaders as one of the biggest hurdles we must overcome. Allow me to explain a bit further.

**Raising Up a New Breed of Patriot Leaders**

The times in which we live call for a new breed of patriot leaders to emerge. The recent track record of the freedom movement has only further demonstrated our shortcomings. In general, we are an independent group of rugged individualists, very opinionated and unbridled. We often joke among ourselves that trying to promote unity and cooperation within this movement is like herding cats! As a result, we are very disunited and relatively ineffectual.

Those who have aspired to be leaders or spokespersons for our movement have often elevated their message above their character or example. Again, the results have not been that positive. When we interact with our fellow Americans or argue our points without people skills, patience and diplomacy, we are often surprised when others do not automatically grasp what we are saying. We alienate others with our mannerisms and behavior, and frequently cause them to marginalize our movement because they perceive us to be 'right wing nuts.'

Even when relating to others who are sympathetic within our own movement, we often portray inflated egos and very little flexibility or willingness to cooperate. We compete with each other and constantly divide over the smallest of issues. We shoot our own wounded and quickly abandon our own comrades if they falter. In short, there are far too many 'leaders,' and not nearly enough followers.

If we are to restore our Republic, we must see a breakthrough in the caliber of our leadership. I pray frequently for the raising up of this new breed of leaders, who will lead us by example and inspire us to find a way together to save our nation.

I have identified five essential qualities for this new breed of patriot leaders. I trust this will help to illustrate my point.

1. Inward – Honest, loyal, humble and teachable
2. Outward – Personable, disciplined, reliable, persevering and tenacious
3. Vision - Sees the big picture and the steps to get there
4. Passion - Deep conviction and burning zeal
5. Interdependent - Flexible, balanced, a true team player

**The Urgency of Our Times**

A narrow focus will hinder us from correctly prioritizing our daily priorities and activities. When we lack a sense of urgency, we can easily become distracted or embedded in activities and causes that by themselves will not enable us to achieve victory. By way of contrast, a clear focus and sense of urgency will force us to identify root issues and then form calculated responses. We must adjust to this new way of thinking (and soon), for our previous methods have not turned the tide.

We live in urgent times, folks. We can no longer afford to waste time fighting little wildfires when the whole forest is about to be engulfed in flame. Or, as one of my good friends illustrates from the example of 9/11, we cannot focus on putting out office fires in the twin towers when the whole building is about to come down.

Our movement needs a major paradigm shift, one that lines up with the actual threat levels that we face presently. We have seen the positive affects as people have stood up in mass to protest. As we proceed forward, the emergence of this new breed of patriot leaders will guide us to victory. However, if we do not make these adjustments soon, we may very well witness the final demise of our Constitutional Republic.

# Chapter Eight

# Resistance to Tyranny

For many Americans, using the word tyranny in the same sentence as the United States is inconceivable. We honestly do not want to believe that something could be so wrong here in America, so we tend to ignore the ever-increasing warning signs. While carrying on with our busy lives, we fail to heed the many symptoms that point to a serious national epidemic.

**Opposing Tyranny in the United States**

The United States of America is facing unprecedented perils and a critical decline in our unique heritage, culture and form of government. This book is an urgent call for Americans to take a firm stand against the forces, both foreign and domestic, that threaten our future. By now, it should be obvious that the normal channels for change - our government, politics, elections and the media - have become so controlled, self-seeking and corrupt that they no longer represent the original vision or intent of our Founding Fathers. Moreover, many freedom-loving, patriotic Americas are now being labeled as dissidents, potential enemies of the state, or 'domestic terrorists.' In this state of total disarray, any realistic way of holding on to the founding principles of our Republic is fleeting rapidly.

Today we find ourselves, just like our Founding Fathers, in the midst of a serious struggle for freedom and the future of our Republic. We now face the agonizing choice between submitting to corruption and tyranny, and the relinquishment of our essential, unalienable rights and liberties. For us, the choice has become clear, and we have no other recourse but to actively resist those who ignore and refuse to uphold the Constitution and are determined to reshape our nation into something entirely different.

### The Proper Role of Government

The essential nature and purpose of American government is to secure and protect the God-given rights of its citizens. Government exists and functions solely for this purpose. Our Founding Fathers clearly understood the evil tendencies of men, and they knew that governments would inevitably be a reflection of those tendencies. Left unchecked, the tyranny of human government will continue to grow and consume the resources and liberties of the people.

### Our Cause and Struggle

Those early American patriots believed that man possessed unalienable rights from our Creator, and that it was the inherent right of the people to ultimately decide and direct their own lives. It was their distinct understanding that our American form of government would thrive and succeed only with the consent of those who were governed. In their resistance to the tyranny of the British Crown, these brave patriots held firm to the idea that it was the right and responsibility of American citizens to question or challenge their government. Moreover, if necessary, to alter or abolish that government in pursuit of another one that would truly represent their values. Once again, this sentiment was clearly articulated in the Declaration of Independence:

> That whenever any Form of Government becomes destructive of these ends, it is the Right of the People to alter or to abolish it, and to institute new Government . . .

Our cause is firmly rooted in America's own history and quest for independence. This same struggle resurfaced less than a hundred years into our nations' history, when the Southern States chose to secede from the United States in pursuit of their own independence. Eventually squelched in their so-called 'rebellion,' the rights of people and the States were forever altered and subjugated to a more centralized federal government. From that point onward, we have witnessed the gradual and systematic erosion of our liberties, along with the relentless growth and intrusion of government into our lives. Recent events have led us now to the brink of disaster, a point of no return.

Unfortunately, these changes have taken place very gradually (and often secretly), so that the American people would accept and grow accustomed to them. Through shifts in our culture and the manipulation of events, we have allowed ourselves to become what we once despised. Our nation has shifted dramatically toward secularism and socialism. The leaders of both major political parties seem determined to sell out America to globalism and ultimately create a totalitarian state. Along the way, they will sacrifice our liberties, our Judeo-Christian heritage and our national security or sovereignty.

Our cause, therefore, is to restore the vision and principles of our Founding Fathers. As they confronted, challenged and eventually defeated the greatest empire on earth at that time, so we too must develop a similar conviction, courage and resolve today. It is imperative that we find a way to unite all like-minded individuals and groups for this common cause, and to this end, we now strive.

## Awakening the American People

Most leaders and groups within the freedom movement have correctly identified educating the American people as our highest objective. Yet for all the efforts and progress in this area, we have still failed to reach the masses necessary to affect real change. Perhaps we have underestimated the strength of our adversaries, or the system that they have created to influence the minds of the people.

For many years now, I have been involved in teaching, challenging and motivating people. The past few years, this has spilled over into the political arena, as I myself have learned the truth about what is happening in America. I am sure many of you would find your own life converging into this same path, perhaps from different directions.

I have had the privilege of meeting many fine patriots along the way, as well as others who fit the bill as extremists and wackos of every type. Unfortunately, these few often give the wider group a bad name and inhibit the process of educating the American people in the principles of liberty. While always striving to remain open-minded to new information, I have chosen nonetheless to identify myself primarily with those who maintain a sense of balance and reason in their approach. I do this because I want to remain in touch with the average American on the street. I have found that most Americans are incapable of understanding and digesting the massive amounts of information that well-meaning 'patriots' often try to thrust upon them. Our failure to articulate and dispense information to our fellow citizens in understandable, bite-sized pieces has been one of our biggest problems.

## An Urgent Call to the Patriot Community

Confronted with a multitude of imminent threats to our Constitutional Republic, those of us who have been awakened to the plight of our nation face one preeminent obstacle. As serious as the many external pressures are, there is one threat even greater. Within the freedom movement, we are disunited and therefore relatively weak and ineffectual in resisting the ever-encroaching tyranny of our government here in America. For the most part, we are also ill prepared for the imminent crisis which is about to engulf our nation.

I believe that the answer to this dilemma is to network and build coalitions, whereby we can increase our effectiveness through cooperation and synergism. The best place to do this is in our own communities and in our own states.

## Forming Patriot Coalitions and Communities

I firmly believe that America is at a real crossroads, and we must respond accordingly at the local and state level. This can best be done by encouraging unity and collaboration between the like-minded patriot groups that already exist. At the same time, this may be our biggest challenge, because we tend to be a very independent, strong-willed group of people - not often humble, teachable or willing to cooperate. We are frequently not able to grasp the big picture, because we are so narrowly embedded in a particular issue or crusade.

In my opinion, those who possess the rare qualities of humility, diplomacy and a broader vision will become the strong leaders that this movement needs. People who have the necessary experience and people skills to build these bridges will rise unselfishly to the surface for the cause of liberty.

Here in New Mexico, we have formed a group called the 'New Mexico Patriot Alliance,' which focuses squarely on these objectives. There may be a coalition like this in your state already. You should get involved, or if there is not a group like this, consider starting one. Do not hesitate or procrastinate – we do not have time.

**A Proposal for Your Consideration**

The formation of unified patriot communities at the local and state levels will provide not only mutual support, but will also enable us to prepare for what appears to be on the horizon in America. As most citizens are woefully ignorant or indifferent to what is going on, it is imperative that we do this NOW, so that we will be able to help many others later. I submit for your consideration these primary objectives:

- That we continue our efforts in the various groups that we represent.
- That we cooperate with one another instead of remaining isolated or distant.
- That we identify common or shared values and rally around those principles.
- That we form a broad-based coalition built on these shared values.
- That we develop a functional network for mutual care, training and mobilization.

To this, I would add the following suggested goals:

- Formation of steering committees to chart the course of these networks.
- Cross-pollination and collaborative efforts between various groups.
- Develop strategic plans for patriot education, crisis preparedness and training.
- Form localized, small groups to facilitate and achieve these goals.
- Strengthen and expand these alliances across our states.

Building statewide patriot communities will be the key to our strategy for restoring America. By forming strong coalitions and preparing ourselves, we will be better equipped to handle any further onslaught of tyranny.

**Our Mission**

As declining trends become clearer on the horizon, it is crucial that Americans wake up and take a determined stand together for liberty. I am convinced that the majority of Americans are asleep, unaware and thoroughly ill equipped for this impending crisis. We are running out of time and must no longer be passive spectators. Now is the time for passion, courage and action!

Within these patriot communities, there should be two intertwining missions. Our overall purpose is to provide an opportunity for concerned Americans to become actively involved in the process of restoring our Republic. We acknowledge that there are numerous other groups across America focused on one or more of the same issues or goals, and we will strive to network or build bridges of unity and cooperation with all such persons and groups. We will consider any person or group that shares our basic values, and who is aligned with the Constitution, to be our friend or ally. We do so, believing that unity is essential for the achieving of our goals and objectives. Our only hope for restoring America is through this type of unity and coordinated efforts!

At the personal or local level, our purpose will be to prepare ourselves for the troubled times that are coming upon America. By networking together, we will refuse to remain ignorant or unprepared. Our primary objectives will be to alert, educate, train and mobilize American citizens, rekindling a spirit of true patriotism and liberty. We will prepare ourselves in practical ways to face the future, and at the same time, we will strive to build bridges of cooperation with other like-minded patriots who share the same concerns and values. To these ends, our vision is to create such awareness among the American population that our call for restoration will be heard, affecting a lasting change in our government!

**On the Operational Front**

These state alliances should operate on several fronts in their struggle to restore America. Reaching and educating the American people is essential to our cause, so we will work to build a grass roots movement through personal contact and increased public awareness.

We must strive to form crossover networks with other like-minded patriot groups, to fan the flames of liberty and to stimulate greater unity and synergy with our efforts. Our coalitions will promote the education, recruitment and training of true American patriots. We will mobilize the people to question and challenge current government ethics and policies. We will engage the people and the government on the streets, in the political arena and in the courts. We will endeavor to increase public awareness and media coverage by targeting individuals and issues that are blatantly unconstitutional and unethical.

At the local level, our alliances will also represent a tangible form of preparation and training by creating a vibrant patriot community that will facilitate mutual care, communication and coordinated efforts. This focus will include education, personal support and crisis preparedness.

**Get Involved Now**

If you share these concerns and see the need to do something about it, now is the time to get involved! Local groups are undoubtedly forming now in your area. We invite you to become part of this growing patriot community, helping us to preserve and restore America to the principles and values that made us the strongest nation on earth.

## Understanding the Times

It is widely accepted that the United States is the final bastion of liberty in the world. However, as the pressure mounts to deal with vast, complex global problems, America is viewed increasingly with contempt or as an obstacle to worldwide solutions. Even those within our own government seem determined to dilute our unique heritage and sovereignty, choosing instead to steer us into conformity with the global community. As they seek to both survive and reshape America, they do so by taking a lower position, rather than leading the world by example, character and strength.

Like a rapidly spreading wildfire, men and women across this great land are catching fire with a renewed passion to restore America to her former greatness. They are persons, like those of old, "who understood the times and knew what Israel should do," as they gathered around David to restore their nation (I Chronicles 12:32). May this ever-growing band continue to inspire Americans to reclaim their heritage.

## World Government on the Horizon

Developing trends and scenarios will soon bring about increased clamoring for worldwide stabilization and control. This will lead to the restructuring of national alliances, trade agreements, international banking and other global political arrangements. The time may not be far off when the unthinkable may take place once again.

> Hitler, I believe, is a prototype of the Antichrist who will someday arise and perform economic and political wonders. He too, will mesmerize

> millions and demand the worship of the world. He will be able to accomplish feats of conquest and control that Hitler could not have dreamed possible. – Erwin Lutzer, *Hitler's Cross*

Those with foresight should respond now to the trends of globalization that will eventually set the stage for the emergence of a diabolical world leader, who will represent an elite group of power hungry individuals.

**Alter or Abolish?**

The Declaration of Independence clearly empowers We the People to hold our government accountable for how they lead the nation. Our forefathers believed that it was not only their right, but also their duty! If the government drifted too far, or failed repeatedly and deliberately to act as true representatives of the people, then the people would have every right to either alter or even abolish that form of government. In our case presently, it is not so much a matter of overthrowing or replacing our government, but rather restoring it to the original vision and intent of our Founding Fathers.

> Simply put, the Declaration of Independence states that the people, if they find that their basic rights are being systematically attacked by the state, have a duty to try to change that government, and if they cannot do so, to abolish it. – Francis Schaeffer, *A Christian Manifesto*

The recent Continental Congress 2009 gathered in the same manner as in the early days of our nation, with a sincere desire to achieve these goals. After years of exposing and challenging unconstitutional government practices, interlaced with appeals, declaration of grievances, legal filings and court cases, citizen-delegates from each of the states assembled to discuss the future of our nation and to deliberate on an appropriate course of action. Following in the footsteps of the colonial Continental Congress, first assembled in 1774, these delegates wrestled with similar issues that now threaten the very future of our Republic. Their collaborative efforts resulted in *The Articles of Freedom*, which are now being circulated widely to gain the support of the American people. Having been ignored, abused and shuffled away for long enough, the people once again have begun to rise in unison, demanding lawful, ethical representation and the upholding of our Constitution.

> In Defense of a Free People, the time has come to reassert our God-Given, Natural Rights and cast off tyranny…
>
> Let the Facts Reveal: The federal government of the United States of America was instituted to secure the Individual Rights of our citizens and instead now threatens our Life, Liberty and Property through usurpations of the Constitution. Emboldened by our own lack of responsibility and due diligence in these matters, government has exceeded its' mandate and abandoned those Founding Principles which have made our nation exceptional;
>
> Our servant government has undertaken these unconstitutional actions in direct violation of their enumerated duties, to the detriment of the People's liberty and the sovereignty of our Republic;
>
> Over many years and spanning multiple political administrations, the People who have, in good conscience, attempted to deliberate our grievances and voice our dissent against these offensive

actions through both Petition and Assembly, have been maligned and ignored with contempt;

The People of the several States of Alabama, Alaska, Arizona, Arkansas, California, Colorado, Connecticut, Delaware, Florida, Georgia, Hawaii, Idaho, Illinois, Indiana, Iowa, Kansas, Kentucky, Louisiana, Maine, Maryland, Massachusetts, Michigan, Minnesota, Mississippi, Missouri, Montana, Nebraska, Nevada, New Hampshire, New Jersey, New Mexico, New York, North Carolina, Ohio, Oregon, Pennsylvania, Rhode Island, South Carolina, South Dakota, Tennessee, Texas, Utah, Vermont, Virginia, Washington, West Virginia, Wisconsin and Wyoming, justly alarmed at these arbitrary and unconstitutional actions, have met as Citizen-Delegates, and sat in a general Congress, in the city of St. Charles, Illinois;

Whereupon We, as these Citizen-Delegates, have gathered in defense of Divine Justice, Liberty and the principles of limited government, now stand in clear recognition of the Supreme Law of the Land – the Constitution for the United States of America;

Therefore, we demand that Government immediately re-establish Constitutional Rule of Law, lest the People be forced to do so themselves; and we hereby serve notice that in the Defense of Freedom and Liberty there shall be NO COMPROMISE to which we shall ever yield.

- From the *Articles of Freedom*, Declaration and Resolves of Continental Congress 2009

As determined and passionate as their predecessors, these modern day patriots have now laid their lives on the line to restore America. Make no mistake - we are reliving a drama that began in colonial America. The verdict is still out; the outcome of this chapter has yet to be written. Yet one thing is for sure – liberty beats strongly in the hearts of a remnant of people who will not yield to control, oppression and tyranny!

**Rebuilding America – Starting Now**

While it may be difficult for some to grasp, it is nonetheless crucial to comprehend the need to rebuild America. We must begin doing so now, not at some undetermined or distant point in the future. If we wait much longer, the window of opportunity will be slammed in our faces.

What do I mean by 'rebuilding America?' First, as unpleasant as it is, this process requires first tearing down strongholds that have been built over the years to sidetrack or destroy the original intent of our Founding Fathers. This would translate into a massive downsizing of both federal and state governments. It would also include true fiscal responsibility, breaking the stranglehold of our so-called two-party political system, election and tax reform, cutting off the growing trends of socialism, corporate and special interests, the transfer of American jobs and assets to foreigners, and all participation in political or economic schemes of globalization. We must demand ethical behavior from our leaders and either remove or prosecute those who will not comply and uphold their oath to the Constitution of the United States of America.

In the days to come, following through with this course of action will result in counter pressure and stiffer reprisals from the government. As tyranny is exposed, it always reacts with stronger measures to silence and subdue its opponents. We must realize the nature of the beast and be prepared to face whatever comes, and for however long, in order to bring down this monster. Bringing tyrants out of their lair into full view will also result in more and more people realizing what they are doing. Throughout this process, we must continue on, while clinging to the belief that in the end, good will triumph over evil.

# Chapter Nine

# Civil Disobedience

One of the primary methods of resistance to tyranny is civil disobedience. This type of action involves an active refusal to obey certain laws or demands of a government or occupying foreign power. A calculated form of resistance to tyranny, this approach is primarily nonviolent, more of an expression of respectful disagreement; a sincere appeal to influence those in power to readjust their unjust or unlawful practices.

Protests of this nature typically involve boycotts, public demonstrations, marches, blockades, hunger fasts and other forms of dissent. This basic philosophy of non-cooperation may also include war protests, a refusal to pay taxes or otherwise support the existing powers. Persons who engage in these activities possess a strong resistance mentality, which means remaining firm, not complying or retaliating even when being persecuted or attacked.

Civil disobedience has been advocated and practiced with varying degrees of success throughout history. During the Protestant Reformation period, many utilized civil protest against state controlled churches. One of the earliest modern mass movements of civil disobedience was conducted by the Egyptians against the British in their nonviolent rebellion of 1919. Other movements in Czechoslovakia, East Germany, Pakistan, South Africa, the Baltic nations and more recently in the Ukraine and Georgia have all enabled the people to break free from the shackles of unjust rulers.

**America Draws from the Trailblazers**

Those who had blazed the trail of liberty in Europe shaped the views of the early American colonists. Allow me to give you few examples.

John Knox was a Scottish clergyman who developed a theology of resistance to tyranny. He became one of the foremost leaders of the Protestant Reformation. Knox maintained that the common people had a right to disobedience and rebellion if state officials ruled contrary to the higher laws of God. His tenacious, outspoken views sprang from a belief that it was our duty to resist unethical or unjust rulers. He courageously exposed and reprimanded those of nobility. Often chastised and exiled, his voice continued on long after he died.

Samuel Rutherford was also a Scottish theologian and political activist. His epic work entitled *Lex Rex: the Law and the Prince*, presented a theory of limited government and constitutionalism. This work sent shock waves throughout Europe in the seventeenth century. His primary challenge was to the basic premise of governments at that time, known as 'the divine right of kings.'

> This doctrine held that the king or state ruled as God's appointed regent, and, this being so, the king's word was law. Placed against this position was Rutherford's assertion that the basic premise of civil government, and therefore law, must be based on God's law as given in the Bible. As such, Rutherford argued, all men, even the king, are under the Law and not above it.
> - Francis Schaeffer, *A Christian Manifesto*

Rutherford also held strong convictions regarding the right to resist unlawful authority. His work and life challenged the status quo and propelled the cause of liberty.

> It follows from Rutherford's thesis that citizens have a moral obligation to resist unjust and tyrannical government.
> – Francis Schaeffer, *A Christian Manifesto*

Others, like Martin Luther, John Calvin, William Tyndale and John Bunyan, took an unwavering stand against tyranny, even when it was cloaked in religion. We dare not forget their courage and sacrifice as we face the same type of enemies today.

John Locke, an English philosopher and physician, later secularized many of Rutherford's ideas. In his writings, Locke outlined four basic principles that later became ingrained in the minds of the framers of our Republic. Those points, clearly identifiable in our founding documents, are:

- Inalienable rights
- Government by consent
- Separation of powers
- The right to resist unlawful authority

> The bottom line is that at a certain point there is not only the right, but the duty, to disobey the state… In almost every place where the Reformation had success there was some form of civil disobedience or armed rebellion.
> – Francis Schaeffer, *A Christian Manifesto*

**An Alternative to War Emerges**

Following the Peterloo Massacre in England in 1819, a political poem entitled *The Mask of Anarchy* proposed a radically new form of social action - nonviolent protest. In America, Henry David Thoreau took up the torch with his popular 1849 essay *Civil Disobedience* (originally titled *Resistance to Civil Government*), which embodied the same principles of nonviolent protest. Thoreau's driving idea was that people should be self-reliant and actively refuse to support the government, without necessarily having to fight against it physically. In his essay, Thoreau articulated his personal reasons for refusing to pay taxes and his strong protest of both slavery and the Mexican-American War.

Years later, Mahatma Gandhi developed *Satyagrah*, a system of passive resistance, which was employed extensively in South Africa and India. Gandhi's theories later greatly influenced Nelson Mandela in the struggle against apartheid in South Africa and Martin Luther King in the Civil Rights Movement in the United States.

In response to challenges made by advocates of violence, Mahatma Gandhi once said:

> I do believe that, were there is only a choice between cowardice and violence, I would advise violence... I would rather have India resort to arms in order to defend her honor than that she should, in a cowardly manner, become or remain a helpless witness to her own dishonour ... But I believe that nonviolence is infinitely superior to violence, forgiveness is more manly than punishment.

**The Civil Rights Movement in America**

In order to eradicate the lingering effects of slavery and segregation in America, a movement took hold in the 1960s under the leadership and inspiration of Dr. Martin Luther King,

Jr., a Baptist minister, superb orator and social activist. King worked tirelessly to challenge and inspire the people of the United States. He fought against racial discrimination and poverty, while protesting both segregation and the Vietnam War.

As mentioned before, Martin Luther King was deeply influenced by Mahatma Gandhi's approach to peaceful resistance.

> Like most people, I had heard of Gandhi, but I had never studied him seriously. As I read I became deeply fascinated by his campaigns of nonviolent resistance. I was particularly moved by his Salt March to the Sea and his numerous fasts. The whole concept of Satyagraha (Satya is truth which equals love, and agraha is force; Satyagraha, therefore, means truth force or love force) was profoundly significant to me. As I delved deeper into the philosophy of Gandhi, my skepticism concerning the power of love gradually diminished, and I came to see for the first time its potency in the area of social reform... It was in this Gandhian emphasis on love and nonviolence that I discovered the method for social reform that I had been seeking. – Martin Luther King, Jr.

Dr. King rallied African-Americans by implementing the same principles of nonviolent civil disobedience, and was therefore successful in breaking these strongholds. From the steps of the Lincoln Memorial during a march in 1963, King reminded the crowd of over 200,000 persons:

> In a sense we've come to our nation's capital to cash a check. When the architects of our republic wrote the magnificent words of the Constitution and the Declaration of Independence, they were signing a promissory note to which every

> American was to fall heir. This note was a promise that all men - yes, black men as well as white men - would be guaranteed the unalienable rights of life, liberty and the pursuit of happiness. It is obvious today that America has defaulted on this promissory note, insofar as her citizens of color are concerned. Instead of honoring this sacred obligation, America has given the Negro people a bad check; a check which has come back marked 'insufficient funds' …

Unfortunately, despite his message of love and peaceful protest, Martin Luther King, just as Mahatma Gandhi before him, was eventually assassinated. Their legacies continue as a testament of the use of nonviolent, indirect force to reestablish liberty and justice.

## The Fourth Branch of Government

You could easily say therefore, that 'We the People' are actually the fourth branch of government here in the United States. If the other three branches become corrupted or tyrannical, then our only remaining hope is that the people themselves will come to their senses and rise up to restore our nation. In reality, if We the People had not abdicated our responsibility over the past 100 years, our situation would not have become this bad.

When the people of America assume their rightful place, refusing to be bullied or intimidated further, then our government will once again be held in check and perform as it is supposed to. If we do not, we will be subject to whatever chains are imposed upon us, our children, and our grandchildren.

**The Bottom Line**

Civil disobedience is an integral part of restoring our liberty here in the United States. We are well past the appeal or petitioning stage, my friends. Those in power must hear the voice and will of the people. Let us do whatever is necessary to make sure that this happens.

> For the Founding Fathers, the bottom line was not an abstract point over a tea table; at a certain point it had to be acted upon. The thirteen colonies reached the bottom line: they acted in civil disobedience. That civil disobedience led to open war in which men and women died. And that led to the founding of the United States of America. – Francis Schaeffer, *A Christian Manifesto*

# Chapter Ten

# Weathering the Storm

> A prudent man sees danger and takes refuge, but the simple keep going and suffer for it.
> - Proverbs 22:3, NIV

A storm is gathering – the perfect storm, one that has been building and gaining strength for many years. It now looms on the world's horizon, threatening life and civilization, as we know it. For all true American patriots, the critical issue is how we respond personally to these developments. We may choose to either ignore the cataclysmic chaos that is coming or brace ourselves and prepare for the storm. A fool will ignore, pretend or lie to himself, thinking that disaster will never come close to his house. Those who possess wisdom and foresight will see what is coming and take measures to protect themselves.

Although even more true today, consider these thoughts, penned in 1980:

> Today we are on the brink of a worldwide crisis. Exactly how this crisis will unfold and what each of us will encounter is uncertain. The effects will vary from place to place. But, unquestionably, life for us will be different – in some ways, radically different. – Jim Durkin, *The Coming World Crisis*

In the very near future America may face unimaginable events – such as financial collapse, food or fuel shortages, mass demonstrations, riots, looting, chaos, violence and possibly martial law or war on our own soil. What will you do if these events should occur? Or perhaps a better question is - what will you do now to prepare for these events?

**Preparing Ourselves**

In light of the very real and imminent crises facing America, those who refuse to be fools need to prepare themselves now. Ignoring the signs or procrastinating will only leave us short on time later. When everything hits the fan, it will be too late to come up with a plan, or help others at that time. We would be thrust into survival mode, incapable of doing anything to resolve the problems. It is far better to wake up and prepare now, so that later we are not merely reacting to the circumstances around us.

The alternatives to being prepared for impending crisis would be to remain asleep or to be led exactly where those in power wish us to go. Your personal liberty will be dramatically reduced by events beyond your imagination, and unless you have developed contingency plans, it will be extremely difficult to respond with anything but a self-focused, survivalist mentality.

**Beyond Self-Centeredness**

Many who read this book will be tempted to respond with a focus on self-preservation only. This is the easiest, most natural path, and many will yield to its strong magnetic pull. To do this, however, will simply delay our suffering and protect us for only a few insignificant moments longer. Then we will be all alone, facing the full brunt of the storm by ourselves. Personally, I decided some time ago that this option was not only unacceptable, but also very narrow and selfish.

Even though it is important to take care of ourselves, and those close to us, stopping there would only expose a self-centered approach to life. This is not the spirit that gave birth to

America or made us strong as a nation. We must realize this and resist the temptation, so that future generations of Americans will be able to continue experiencing the blessings of our way of life.

Writing to a Christian audience, pastor and author Jim Durkin goes on to say:

> If your convictions are shaped by whether or not people think what you are doing is strange – instead of being shaped by God's word and its principles – you will ultimately find that many of your convictions are weak and formless… We can prepare ourselves to take full advantage of the unique and unprecedented opportunities for God's kingdom that will appear in the troubled years ahead. Or we can divert our lives to the lesser aim of personal survival.
> – Jim Durkin, *The Coming World Crisis*

**Taking Practical Steps Now**

In the early days of our Republic, the American colonists formed what were called 'Committees of Safety.' These groups were created with a purpose of resisting tyranny through cooperation and personal preparedness. Today, in many places around the country, similar groups are beginning to emerge, as people sense imminent danger and crisis. These groups are encouraging people in basic preparedness matters, such as developing contingency plans, storing food and water, purchasing firearms and ammunition, and finding alternatives for securing other supplies and medical care. In addition, people are learning how to live debt-free, secure their assets, invest in gold or silver, and use barter systems and alternative currencies for trade. Some are exploring ways to get 'off the grid' as much as possible. Encouraging mutual care and self-sufficiency is one of the strongest ways we can prepare ourselves at the personal level.

Developing strategies for community and self-reliance will be our best chance for surviving the coming storm together. Lifestyle changes never come easy, yet with courage and determination we can face the realities of our changing world and adapt ourselves before it is too late. Please start today to develop a personal plan. There are others who will help and support you. Do not allow yourself to be lulled back to sleep.

Take steps now to evaluate your own situation personally. Identify those in your circle of influence (family, friends and other acquaintances) who would be supportive or at least open-minded to these ideas. Check around your local area to see if other like-minded patriots are already pursing these goals, and then work together to develop your own strategies and contingency plans. Most importantly, get involved with a local support group, or start one. Do it now – waiting will only reduce the amount time you have to prepare.

**Forming Networks and Coalitions**

Confronting the huge, complex problems of our nation seems completely overwhelming to most people. We must take a smaller bite. Forming localized support groups and networking across your state are the most effective ways to do this.

As mentioned previously, here in New Mexico we have started a coalition called the *New Mexico Patriot Alliance*, which has endeavored to create a unified support network of like-minded people around our state. This renewed emphasis on cooperation and community, with neighbors helping one another, will be a welcome and long overdue response to a culture that has been gradually stripped of most personal interaction. Hopefully, similar groups are forming in other states and at some point we can link up with each other to help defend ourselves and restore our Constitutional Republic.

## Identifying the Trigger Points

Discerning patriots, who are wisely preparing, should also identify potential events that would indicate a societal meltdown and thereby trigger an escalalated response on our part. These scenarios could come from a multitude of directions – whether it is natural or man-made disasters, financial or governmental collapse, war or invasion, or some series of orchestrated events devised to bring us closer to the New World Order.

On the practical side, these trigger points may also involve food or water shortages, health epidemics, rationing or controlled supply of resources, confiscation of firearms or other property, marshal law and further restrictions on our rights to free speech, assembly, or travel. Any proposed control or taxation of the internet, increased stringency in government-controlled identification, or the targeting and persecution of dissidents, would also be major indicators that totalitarianism is at our doorstep.

## Ever Vigilant

We will no longer yield to media deception, contrived emergencies, and the fear tactics so frequently utilized by our government throughout history. We will be on the lookout for any purported, deceptive plan to enslave us further, even if it appears to be necessary or reasonable on the surface.

Ever awake and vigilant, we will refuse to sit by quietly, but instead we will rise up for the cause of liberty, exposing the tyrants who wish to oppress and use us for their own ends. We will prepare and survive the storm that is coming – and on the other side of the storm, we will remain free!

# Chapter Eleven

# The Patriot Response

**First and Foremost – It's Personal**

As we face the unchartered waters of America's future, it is imperative that we reevaluate many of our personal convictions and priorities. Circumstances require that we do some serious soul searching and sort through the issues that are really important to us. We must find a way to differentiate between personal preferences and base line values. Many issues tend to divide the patriot community, but we must strive to overcome these obstacles by finding common ground and then focusing together on the most important concerns.

On a personal level, I challenge you to rethink the way that you spend the bulk of your available time for the cause of liberty. I have found that many so-called patriots frequently engage in efforts that produce little results. For many, this includes endless talk and debate, internet surfing, circulating emails and contacting their 'representatives,' activities that are quite inadequate for producing any lasting change, especially in light of the urgency of our times. Please don't get me wrong – there is some value to these activities. What is desperately lacking and needed in this hour, however, is the type of personal networking and grass roots interaction that will mobilize the American people for real change.

**Drawing a Line in the Sand**

As we face mounting pressure to change or conform to the 'new America' that is being thrust upon us, we will eventually find ourselves confronted with personal choices and decisions.

Each of us will have to determine where to draw a line in the sand. Will we draw that line over increased taxation, illegal searches or seizures, invasion of our privacy, further infringements upon free speech, travel or our right to bear arms or something else dear to our hearts?

Drawing a line in the sand is a very personal decision. One person's conviction may vary from another's. At the same time, there are several points at which many modern patriots find themselves in complete agreement. May you possess the clarity of thought and inner fortitude to stand firm in your convictions on that day. Standing alone should not be an option for you. Finding and uniting with other patriots in resistance to tyranny should become your pathway and lifestyle from here out.

You must wrestle with many personal decisions in your own response as a patriot living in these perilous times. It is crucial, however, that you work yourself through the process of evaluating and forming solid convictions. No one else can decide for you or give you some magic formula to use in answering these questions. I will not attempt to do that either.

As difficult and painful as it may be, this process will bring you to a point where you know deep inside yourself, which issues are worth living and dying for. This will bring a new perspective and focus to your life, enabling you to readjust your personal priorities. We are living in critical times, and the sooner you embrace this historical and personal reality, the better off you will be.

Once you have determined where you will draw the line in the sand, saying 'no more' to tyrants and their government, you will then need to kick things into high gear. Your response as an American patriot needs to be both decisive and life changing. Anything less will not cut it.

**Resisting Tyranny in Your Front Yard**

Many problems arise when public opinion, petition, or protest falls on deaf ears; or when a government itself becomes compromised and thoroughly corrupt. Most of us would just prefer to be left alone, yet somehow government keeps invading our space, wanting more and more of what we have.

Hiding is not an option either. In our modern world, there are very few frontiers or places left to hide. Finding a place to flee to has become much more difficult than in the days of our ancestors.

When one factors in the energy that patriots have already spent trying to appeal to the government over the course of many years, coupled with the accelerated pace that our leaders are now taking us down the path of socialism and totalitarianism, it should be obvious to all but the uninitiated that we are rapidly approaching a serious conflict. And just like Mel Gibson's movie character, the reluctant "Patriot," who put off personal involvement, this conflict will soon be in your front yard.

> In such an instance, for the private person, for the individual… there are three appropriate levels of resistance: First, he must defend himself by protest (in contemporary society this would most often be by legal action); second, he must flee if at all possible; and third, he may use force, if necessary, to defend himself. One should not employ force if he may save himself by flight; nor should one employ flight if he can save himself and defend himself by protest and the constitutional means of redress.
> – Francis Schaeffer, *A Christian Manifesto*

## Turning Up the Heat

For several generations, good people have generally stood by, watching passively as our Constitution and American values have been gradually stripped away. At this crossroads in history, it is essential that we change this mentality.

> It is important to understand that bringing justice to evildoers and protecting the innocent works in favor of peace. Pacifism merely allows chaos and tyranny to reign. Like a skilled surgeon aggressively pursuing a cancerous tumor, a just and righteous nation will remove the evil that seeks to destroy its people.
> – James Robison, *The Soul of a Nation*

The time has come for the patriot movement to shift into an offensive posture. For years, we have been playing defense, merely reacting to the changes that have been thrust upon us; and we have been losing the game. If we truly wish to restore our Constitutional Republic, we must turn up the heat and begin to put pressure back on the government!

> Do not give in to evil, but proceed ever more boldly against it. - Ludwig von Mises

## Mobilizing the Three Percent

Most of us have been led to believe that we must be in the majority to prevail. Historically, and in truth, change is always affected by a rather small percentage of dedicated, selfless, radical individuals who persevere and will stop at nothing until their objectives are achieved. It has been estimated that American independence was achieved with only about 3-4% of Americans in full support. This changes everything!

## Building a Strong, Unified Patriot Community

Our best hope and the key to victory is the American people. We must educate, unify and mobilize as many patriots as possible in order to mount a counter attack on the true enemies of our Republic.

> To be sure, the U.S. Constitution is not perfect. Few human contrivances are. But it is a pretty good one, I think, and it defines the limits and scope of government… I do not believe that most Americans want to continue down this path: undeclared wars without end, more and more police-state measures, and a Constitution that may as well not exist. But this is not a fated existence. We do not have to live in this kind of America. It is not too late to rally and recall our people to the Constitution, the rule of law, and our traditional American republic.
> – Ron Paul, *The Revolution: A Manifesto*

I firmly believe that if we can get our message to the people, there will be a tremendous awakening and a resurgence of liberty that will overturn all the schemes of America's enemies. Developing a strong, unified patriot community should be our highest priority.

## Mass Protest and Civil Disobedience

With the escalating national crisis, it is becoming apparent that we must up the ante. The time for apathy and timidity has past! We must now hit the government where it hurts, holding them accountable, challenging their decisions at every turn and holding their feet to the fire. The nice guy rules from days gone by have now evaporated into a struggle for the soul and future of our nation.

This conflict has begun already! You have seen the thousands gathered in mass protest on the streets of America, in town hall meetings, and in Washington, D.C. This is a mere foreshadowing of what is to come – in the very near future. Protest and civil disobedience will undoubtedly evoke a further response from the government, and eventually this will expose their motives and the tyranny that resides in their hearts.

Hitting the government where it hurts is plain and simple. While bailing out their cronies, they require more and more of our hard-earned money to operate. By withholding our financial support, we can become a powerful mass movement that sends a clear message: NO MORE. We must stop feeding the beast that is devouring our Republic and our future.

Is this radical? Of course. Is this response needed now? Yes. Are we serious about saving our nation? I hope you get the point.

## The Option of Secession

One movement that has gained traction recently is related to the Tenth Amendment and the sovereignty of the States here in America. This issue was central to the struggle of our American Civil War and has now come to the forefront again as the federal government continues to grow and impose its will upon the several States.

For nearly the first half of our nation's history, the right to govern at the State level, as well as the concept of secession, were universally understood and accepted. Today, quite a number of States are reasserting this fundamental right and standing up to the Feds. This trend will most likely continue as the crisis and pressure to conform grows stronger. For some States, this may inevitably lead to a very real effort to secede from the union. This would involve the dissolution of a voluntary contract with the federal government, just as our Founding Fathers did in response to the king of England. A truly free people should be allowed to do so, and not be held captive through financial blackmail or by gunpoint.

> One need look no further than the Declaration of Independence for exposition of a 'moral' right to secede, which every single one of the colonies acknowledged by signing the document… In other words, the right to secede from any confederation, group, or union is derived from the Natural Law of freedom to associate.
> - Andrew Napolitano, *The Constitution in Exile*

**Reinstating the Constitutional Militia**

In an effort to connect all the dots and formulate a plan for victory, I have realized that we also need to consider the basic issue of our personal and corporate self-defense. The natural right to keep and bear arms and to band together in defense of our families and communities was upheld in our founding documents.

Even though most people are afraid to talk about it, we must now consider the need to revitalize the constitutionally based citizen's militia. Ever mindful of how to manipulate public opinion, the government paints a distinct picture of the 'militia,' by exploiting the weird behavior of a radical fringe element. They are quick to denounce and marginalize, labeling any militias as 'potential domestic terrorists.' The resurgence of the militia movement in the 90's was eventually neutralized using these tactics.

The right of free people to defend themselves is the issue at stake here. Without this right, we are left with absolutely no protection from tyrants. This is American Liberty 101, folks. If the government controls every facet of gun ownership, self-defensive recourse and the militias themselves, they have already stripped us of our God-given rights.

Revitalizing the militia within each State would help to ensure that the people are protected and the Constitution is upheld as the Supreme Law of the Land. Even though the Constitution clearly states that the government is responsible to equip and train the militia, I am NOT referring here to the National Guard or State Guard or other entity controlled by the government. Unfortunately, the narrowness, immaturity, and stigmas attached to the militia movement of the 90's are things we will have to overcome. Nevertheless, this can be done if we have clear objectives and proper, balanced leadership.

**The Use of Force**

During the time of the American Revolution, the colonists were ultimately forced to assume a defensive position to protect their own rights. Appeals, debate and legislation only gave way to further oppression. Eventually, they came to view the British as invaders who were intent on subverting their legitimate colonial governments. The people ultimately had no recourse but either to surrender their liberty or fight to preserve their ideals and way of life. Surely, we once again live in such a time as this.

> If there is a legitimate reason for the use of force, and if there is a vigilant precaution against its overreaction in practice, then at a certain point a use of force is justifiable... In a fallen world, force in some form will always be necessary... Two principles, however, must always be observed. First, there must be a legitimate basis and a legitimate exercise of force. Second, any overreaction crosses the line from force to

> violence. And unmitigated violence can never be justified. – Francis Schaeffer, *A Christian Manifesto*

Many Americans, while upholding a belief in our military system, fall short of embracing their personal right to self-defense against oppression and tyranny. We support the government when they claim to be 'spreading democracy' around the world, or when they claim to be 'fighting for freedom,' yet nothing could be more basic than protecting the liberties and rights of the American people!

We have been duped into thinking that only the government is able to discern right from wrong; or that only the government is endowed with the right to protect us. In short, we have been lulled to sleep! In reality, a government is not a person who is endowed with natural rights by our Creator. A government is an entity created by the people, and as our servants, they are subject to us!

Most Americans are decent, law-abiding people. As such, we are not inclined to violence, and we believe that fighting or war accomplishes very little that is positive. However, we must no longer sit by and refuse to challenge the system that threatens to destroy our nation and our way of life. Any use of force is an unfortunate and historical reality throughout human history. If backed into a corner, my belief is that the American people will fight and not surrender these rights. If we don't, we truly deserve whatever shackles are placed upon us.

> If we make peaceful revolution impossible, we make violent revolution inevitable.
> - President John F. Kennedy

## Taking our Country Back

It has been well said that our Constitution does not defend itself. The people themselves must rise now in its defense! We must determine with deep resolve to do whatever it takes to restore the principles of liberty and to take our nation back.

We live in a critical juncture between our nation's history and its future. Our enemies will not roll over or easily surrender their icy grip on our country. We must believe that freedom is a stronger force; that liberty will prevail over tyranny; and that good will triumph over evil. What else can we do?

## Get on Board Now!

The freedom train has left the station already, but fortunately, there are many stations along the journey to restoring America. There is still plenty of room on board for you. Throw off all ignorance, apathy, and any narrow focus or defeatist mentality. Take your place now with your fellow freedom fighters.

> We are not weak if we make a proper use of those means which the God of Nature has placed in our power... the battle, sir, is not to the strong alone; it is to the vigilant, the active, the brave.
> – Patrick Henry

# Chapter Twelve

# Live Free or Die

We live today in a time that eerily resembles the founding of America. This time however, we are not primarily plagued with an invading or occupying foreign power on our soil, but rather an immense host of our own fellow citizens, who have either forgotten or abandoned our unique American heritage and form of government. To be sure, we have foes in other lands, but the most dangerous enemies we face today are those who live among us; those who claim to be Americans, yet who would sell their souls to the devil or the highest bidder.

It is clear that our Founding Fathers believed that it was an unalienable right, bestowed by our Creator, to resist tyranny and to do whatever was necessary to ensure the perpetuity of liberty in America. As much as we might wish to ignore the facts or hide ourselves from unpleasant realities, it is nevertheless true that we are, in fact, in the middle of a revolution. Some of you are still hesitant to admit or act upon this reality, yet the day is coming soon when the full brunt of this battle for the soul of America and the free world will be upon you.

> The bad guys may win, but I am going to make their lives as miserable as possible before I go. Patrick Henry understood that there are three possibilities:
>
> You can live your life as a free sovereign.
> You can die attempting to protect your freedom.
> You can give up and succumb to slavery.

> Patrick Henry and I refuse to be slaves. That is not an acceptable option.
> - Michael Badnarik, *Good to be King*

**The Sounding of the Trumpet**

You may have rightly discerned that I have written to sound the battle cry of freedom once again. Along with many other patriots, I raise my voice and my heart to the liberation of a people who have been asleep and enslaved for a long time.

Some, who are 'patriots in name only,' will faint at some of the proposals outlined in this book. Many others, whose convictions about liberty are too shallow, will wilt under the pressure of government induced fear and intimidation. A number will choose to argue and debate endlessly, while ignoring the urgency of our times. In addition, not a few will lack the necessary character qualities to be leaders, and their attempt to do so will hamper our efforts. I fully expect all of these situations. Yet still, we must push forward.

When everything hits the fan, these pseudo patriots will never actually cross the line to lay down their lives for the cause of freedom. They talk big, but will disappear quickly when the pressure comes or the fighting begins. They do not have the heart or the courage of true patriots. Therefore, we must be able to recognize persons like this and at least not allow them to be in positions of leadership in our movement. There is too much at stake this time.

Beyond these possible responses, there are still others who will determine in their hearts to stand up for liberty, no matter what the cost. Then, somewhere along the journey, these brave souls will find each other, become unified in purpose and struggle together to restore America.

## The Refiner's Fire

Times like this will test every fiber of our being. Yet we should also be thankful to be alive during a time such as this, when the fate and future of our Republic will be decided. Our second president once gave this sobering reminder:

> People and nations are forged in the fires of adversity. – President John Adams

In the face of overwhelming odds, there is, and always will be, a small group or remnant of deeply committed people who will count the cost and consciously decide to pay whatever price is necessary to secure liberty once again. I am firmly convinced that the American people will follow leaders who will step up to this challenge!

> These are the times that try men's souls. The summer soldier and the sunshine patriot will, in this crisis, shrink from the service of their country; but he that stands it now, deserves the love and thanks of man and woman. Tyranny, like hell, is not easily conquered; yet we have this consolation with us, that the harder the conflict, the more glorious the triumph. – Thomas Paine

## The Patriot's Creed

In early America, newspapers and pamphlets were the primary source of news and information. One important political statement, from an anonymous author, written in a form similar to the *Apostles' Creed*, appeared in the *Massachusetts Spy* on January 19, 1776. It was evidently written the previous year, when many colonists were still taking pains to show their continued loyalty as Englishmen. Read carefully, as it contains the seeds for the justification of what was soon to come in America.

I believe the English Government, such as it appears to have been, from the most unquestioned annals of our country, to be a free constitution of a mixed and limited form; and that its origin is to be sought for, and lies, in the consent of the people.

I believe a King of England has not a claim to absolute, uncontrolled dominion; that if the English government, in its administration, has, at some seasons, been despotic, yet its genius hath at times been free; and that the liberty of the subject, founded upon established laws, was essential to every form under which it appeared.

I believe all political power to be derived originally from, and invested in the people; which power, I believe, they may dispose of, for their own use, in what hands, and under what conditions they please.

I believe a current of liberty has been gradually widening, as well as purifying, in proportion to the distance from its source, a feudal institution; that charters and laws have removed every scruple that might now arise about the reciprocal rights and privileges of the King and his subjects.

I believe the feudal system and absolute dominion, two things perfectly incompatible.

I believe the claim of the Norman Invader to the crown was not conquest but testamentary succession; that he renounced his conquest by a coronation oath; and before he commenced tyrant, confirmed the use of the Saxon laws.

I believe regal power to have no divine right, but to be of human or popular institution; and that the present reigning family's title to the crown, is derived only from parliamentary resolutions, to which revolutionary principles alone gave birth.

I believe passive obedience was not demanded even by Elizabeth or James; nor even acknowledged, by the people, as a matter of right.

I believe legal resistance and rebellion essentially different, and that they originate from quite opposite principles. By the law of nature, every man has a right to defend himself against the abuse of power, and by the singular constitution of this kingdom, when Kings and Ministers; break through the bounds prescribed by the laws, the people's right of resistance is unquestionable.

I believe what is called the English constitution to be that system of government which was first declared by the great charter of England; and after many struggles between the crown and its subjects, was established at the glorious revolution.

I believe I am bound to maintain the Protestant succession as established by law, in the present reigning family, and also to support the Catholic Church of England, so long as it continues united with the state; and therefore I will use my utmost endeavors to oppose the designs of Papists, and every pretender to the throne, as inveterate enemies to both.

I believe a Parliament to be a legislative body, instituted by the people at large with delegated power, intended as a balance between them and the Sovereign; and elected for the sole purposes of preserving their liberties, or defending their lives and estates.

I believe it is my duty to yield an implicit obedience to the laws of my country; that these are a standard of right for both Prince and subject; and that no Englishman ought to suffer in person or property, unless by the uncontrolled judgment of his Peers.

I believe I am under an indispensable obligation to have an eye, in all my pursuits and actions, to peace, safety, and good government; I will, therefore, under God, endeavor to maintain, at all times, true loyalty to my King, and an unfeigned affection to the Magistrate; proportioned to the wisdom and integrity, with which they guard public freedom, and promote national prosperity.

I believe I ought not, on any pretence, to surrender that invaluable liberty, which has been solemnly confirmed to me, by the great transactions of former days; nor to renounce that pure religion which my ancestors sealed with their blood; I will therefore be ready, at any moment, to risk my life in their defence; and so long as I intend fairly and honestly, I trust Almighty God will bless my public and private efforts to advance his glory and my nation's welfare.

- From an *English Patriot's Creed*, Anonymous, 1775, published in Boston, 1776

**Stepping Over the Line**

Today you need to consider seriously the possibilities that lie ahead. Either you will determine in your heart to stand for liberty and truth, or you will ultimately be overrun by tyrannical oppression.

You may be tempted to think that things are not this serious, but I can assure you that this is precisely what our enemies want you to believe. The choice is clearly yours – continue on, sleepwalking and ignoring the truth; or wake up and begin to live free once again.

**Living in Freedom**

Once you have stepped over this line of commitment and made peace with your Creator, you can once again experience the deep, inward peace of true freedom.

Overcoming fear is the key to personal victory. Fear is what holds us back, paralyzes us, and causes us to retreat. Whether trials may come by harassment, persecution, prison or even death, you can still live and die free! They will never be able to take this from you!

When you stand at the end of your life, on the brink of eternity, you can know that you did the right thing. In reality, you can decide right now – in your heart and mind. I urge you today to cross this threshold into a new life of true freedom.

**Free at Last**

The human heart yearns to live and breathe free. Free to think and act according to the dictates of our own beliefs and conscience. Free to pursue all that life and this world have to offer. Free from the manipulation and control of others. We stand together at this time to ensure that the flame of true liberty does not die out in the world.

> Let freedom ring. And when this happens, and when we allow freedom to ring - when we let it ring from every village and every hamlet, from every state and every city, we will be able to speed up that day when all of God's children - black men and white men, Jews and Gentiles, Protestants and Catholics - will be able to join hands and sing in the words of the old Negro spiritual: "Free at last! Free at last! Thank God Almighty, we are free at last!"
> – Martin Luther King, Jr.

**United We Shall Overcome … or Die Trying**

Very few causes in one's lifetime will demand our utmost dedication or sacrifice. Yet we live in such a time today, one that beckons us to take a stand for liberty and the future of our nation.

This unprecedented struggle for liberty and self-determination is also the ultimate clash between all that is good and evil in this world. I pray that you will have the ability to understand and take the right course of action.

> Moreover, believers must never forget that the basis of the state is the power to coerce. The

ultimate sanction behind laws and rules is prison and, in some cases (should you resist), death.
– Michael Cromartie, *Caesar's Coin Revisited*

LIVE FREE OR DIE. Death is not the worst of evils. - General John Stark (this is the State motto of New Hampshire)

LIVE FREE OR DIE … let millions of voices now raise this cry in unison and rescue our land.

Is life so dear or peace so sweet as to be purchased at the price of chains and slavery? Forbid it, Almighty God! I know not what course others may take, but as for me, give me liberty, or give me death! – Patrick Henry

The author would appreciate hearing your comments about this book. Please contact him at dvbatch@gmail.com

# References


The New American Standard Bible
The Declaration of Independence
The Constitution of the United States
The Bill of Rights
A Christian Manifesto – Francis A. Schaeffer
Caesar's Coin Revisited – Edited by Michael Cromartie
Constitutional Homeland Security – Edwin Vieira
Good to Be King – Michael Badnarik
Hitler's Cross – Erwin W. Lutzer
Humanist Manifesto, I, II and III – various authors
Lex Rex, the Law and the Prince – Samuel Rutherford
The 5000 Year Leap – W. Cleon Skousen
The Coming World Crisis – Durkin/Anfuso/Sczepanski
The Communist Manifesto – Karl Marx, Friedrich Engels
The Constitution in Exile – Andrew P. Napolitano
The Federalist Papers – Alexander Hamilton, James Madison, John Jay
The Late, Great USA – Jerome Corsi
The Revolution: A Manifesto – Ron Paul
The Selected Political Writings of John Locke – Edited by Paul E. Sigmund

# About the Author

Like many Americans, Dave Batcheller spent a great portion of his life unaware of America's true history or the deep problems facing our nation. As he approached the age of fifty, he began to connect the dots of our history and the issues threatening America's survival. This led him to the writing of his first book, *The Downward Spiral: Decline of the American Dream.*

Dave was born and raised in Iowa and has lived in several regions of the country. He graduated from Bible College and for many years was involved in church ministry. Along the way, while raising a family, he also worked in a number of other fields; all of which has given him a wide range of experience and interaction with people.

Dave is currently self-employed and resides in New Mexico. He has served as the State Party Chairman for the Constitution Party of New Mexico and is the founder and state coordinator of the New Mexico Patriot Alliance, a group that is on the forefront of efforts to restore liberty and our constitutional form of government here in the United States.

www.ingramcontent.com/pod-product-compliance
Lightning Source LLC
LaVergne TN
LVHW010607160826
845677LV00013B/3292